Living BEYOND DIVORCE

THE POSSIBILITIES OF REMARRIAGE

Jim Smoke

A working guide for *Living Beyond Divorce* is available for individual or group study.

HARVEST HOUSE PUBLISHERS
Eugene, Oregon 97402

Other Books by Jim Smoke:

Every Single Day
Growing Through Divorce
Suddenly Single
Turning Points

LIVING BEYOND DIVORCE

Copyright © 1984 by Harvest House Publishers
Eugene, Oregon 97402

Library of Congress Catalog Card Number 83-082321
ISBN 0-89081-407-4

Printed in the United States of America.

*This book is dedicated
to my sister
Melba
who is learning to
live beyond divorce.*

ACKNOWLEDGMENTS

My thanks to some very special people:

Jeanne, Diana, Ed, Ben, Betty, Delores, Vicki, Sylvia, Carmen, Dana, Jean, Mary, and Barbara.

The thousands of single men and women I have met in my travels across America who have helped me understand what it's like to live in the land beyond divorce.

My secretary and proofreader, Karen Clatanoff.

Special thanks to my friend, Dr. Dwight Small.

CONTENTS

INTRODUCTION

In 1975, when I wrote *Growing Through Divorce*, there was very little in print to guide a person through the wasteland of divorce. In subsequent years, hundreds of books dealing with all aspects of the divorce process have come into print. Every aspect of divorce has been addressed except one. What happens to the person who goes through a divorce experience but is still single five to ten years later?

In conducting Divorce Recovery Seminars across America in the past ten years, I meet more and more divorced men and women who have not remarried. They have shared both their struggles and their joys with me. They have talked about the problems they face and the feelings they experience as single-again persons.

This book acknowledges the feelings and addresses the questions that this special group of people have expressed. Sometimes known as the "silent singles," their divorce has become a distant memory, yet their current existence stirs that memory to life periodically. Their present and future is often tied to their past, but an honest desire to grow and reach their potential can slowly release the strings that tie them to yesterday and can move them toward a fulfilling tomorrow.

This is not a book about the divorcing process. It is a

book about the years of living as a "still-single" person after the divorce wars have ended. Hopefully we can blend many true stories into a fabric of learning and optimism, and say to all who read this book, "It's your life— go for it!"

Jim Smoke
Orange, California

THE QUESTION OF
REMARRIAGE

Every time I conduct a divorce recovery seminar, a few people always come up and ask me what I think about remarriage from a biblical perspective. They often confess their own confusions, having met ministers who will remarry no one who has gone through a divorce, ministers who will remarry some who have gone through a divorce, and ministers who will remarry anyone who has gone through anything.

The purpose of this book is not a theological evaluation of the many differing points of view regarding the right to remarry. Rather, it assumes that each person has come to a conclusion in his own mind that is consistent with the biblical revelation of God and His will for our lives.

For those who are still seeking an answer to the question of remarriage, I usually suggest that a person pray for wisdom and guidance in this area and talk at great lengths with his or her own pastor. It is certainly not an easy question to resolve. Dr. Dwight Small, now retired from the faculty of Westmont College in California, wrote the excellent book *The Right to Remarry* in 1975, an exhaustive research on the subject of remarriage. The *Recommended Reading* at the conclusion of this book can provide additional material to aid in understanding and establishing a biblical perspective.

Chapter 1

Is There
Life After Divorce?

Divorce is like an auto demolition derby. Everyone gathers around to watch it. There is a lot of noise while it is going on. When it is finished, the last car still running gets the prize. The track is covered with the debris of the other cars, and it takes forever to clean up the mess.

The leftover debris from a divorce can often take a lifetime to clean up. The person doing the picking up can often be observed mumbling the words, "Is there really life beyond all this mess?"

Sometimes the leftovers from a divorce appear in a tangible form. They run the gamut from still encountering a former spouse occasionally to dealing with the ongoing child raising process to establishing a new career and meeting economic realities. At other times, the leftovers take on a more intangible appearance. In the quiet hours of the night, when the mind unwinds, questions form about your tomorrows and whether you will share them with a special someone. Should you go it alone and travel light through the rest of you life? Should you keep looking around palm trees and pillars for the great possibility? Should you join a dating service or throw rotten eggs at the one you already tried? Is it safer being alone or should one still venture into the jungle on a regular basis?

Many single-again people have told me they resent having these same questions come up in their consciousness year after year. They want a final resolution rather than a delayed reaction.

The problem with final resolutions is that we are not finished products; we are still being processed through experiences and new growth. Many times when old questions reappear, they are being faced by a new person. Insights will be different. Perspectives will have changed. Feelings and needs will take on a whole new character.

In divorce recovery seminars, we teach the principle that it takes a minimum of two years to work through the basics of your divorce before you are even ready to face the down-the-road questions we have just mentioned. I meet many people who seem to feel the way to resolve a divorce is to meet someone as quickly as possible and remarry. This can become a collision-course relationship that all too easily ends in a second divorce.

In finding out where different people are in their journey through divorce country, I often ask them four questions.

1. Did you avoid your divorce? (Mentally and emotionally)
2. Did you escape your divorce? (Quick new marriage)
3. Did you deny your divorce? (It didn't happen)
4. Did you face your divorce? (Walked through all of it)

I find that many people who have been divorced for long periods of time answer yes on one of the first three questions. There is life beyond divorce, but you have to *work* to get beyond it.

A lady came into my office recently for a counseling appointment. She quickly told me that she did not have any serious problems and that she had been divorced for eight years. Then she looked at me and simply said, "I'm stuck!" Her further comments informed me that she was well beyond her divorce but that she had shriveled up and quit growing in her life. She felt directionless, purposeless, and motionless.

Her situation might well describe yours, mine, and other people's at specific times in life. We all get stuck periodically and we need a few tow trucks in human form to help us break loose. To this woman's credit, she knew where she was and did not want to stay there. Establishing a new life after a divorce is knowing where you are right now and thinking about where you want to go in the future.

Many people who are living beyond their divorce feel there are several stages that they have gone through or are going through in rebuilding their lives. The stages begin at the actual point of divorce and can continue for many years beyond it. I share them with you in the hope that you can identify where you are and know what you are experiencing.

1. *Withdrawal into yourself.* Because of the shame, guilt, and feelings of failure, many people go inside themselves at the beginning of a divorce. In doing this, you can protect yourself from those who would hurt you, but you can also close the door to those who can *help* you. Some aloneness can be therapeutic, but isolation can make you a prisoner to your problems.

2. *Social butterfly.* The reverse of isolation is socialization. The singles' gathering places across our country are populated with newly divorced people who are making

frantic attempts to replace their pain with people. The danger is that hurting people are the most emotionally vulnerable to those who want to help make the hurt go away. Sometimes the giddy feeling of a new freedom coupled with the emotions of a deep hurt can cause you to launch a quest for a person or persons who can inject self-worth and self-esteem back into your life.

People are a vital part of our healing process. Flitting through the singles scene is usually not a healing experience. Instant relationships do not guarantee instant relief.

3. *Stabilization.* You need to find the delicate balance between too few and too many people as you slowly rebuild your postdivorce life. Later in the book we will be talking about building relationships of meaningful significance in your life.

One of the keys of stabilizing your life is feeling good again about yourself. It is knowing who you are and liking it. It is gaining control from the chaos and establishing priorities and goals. It is having the pieces of the puzzle fit without being forced into place. It is walking on the edge without fear of falling off. For many people this comes about the third year after the divorce.

4. *Independence.* You need to learn to fly to new heights on old wings! Many of us were taught to look for the right person to marry when we were growing up. That "right" person was one who could do all the things for us that we could not do for ourselves—one who would take care of us, provide for us, and look after us. It's a good thing that most of us did not tell our dates what we were ultimately looking for in a future husband or wife—they would still be running!

Many people marry into a dependency that never matures into an interdependency. A divorce ultimately forces a person back into taking care of himself and growing into his self-responsibility. Someone has said it wisely in these words: "Always remember, in a divorce you get custody of yourself."

When the spirit of independence rises in postdivorce growth, you will not allow emotional scavengers to raid your life. If you are looking to be looked after, you will short-circuit your growth and the need to build a spirit of independence. In your postdivorce years, your growing independence will enable you to build a better interdependency if you should choose remarriage. More on this in a later chapter.

5. *Where are you? Who needs you?* Somewhere beyond the fifth year after a divorce and a lot of good solid growth and recovery, many people tell me they walk the frustrating line of wondering where the right person for them is hiding (and perhaps after finding one who seems to fill the bill, rejecting the person totally). It almost becomes a song that says, "I want you, I found you, now go away."

There seem to be two fears that are intertwined for single-again persons. The first fear is the fear of never finding the right person for your life. That fear can intensify as one becomes older and the field of prospects narrower. Women over 50 seem to feel very strongly about this. They constantly ask me where all the men in their age bracket can be found. I sometimes answer, "Anchorage, Alaska!" Very few are booked on the next flight, though.

The second fear is the fear of a new marriage not working out and ending the same way as your prior marriage. First-marriage jitters are not the same as second-marriage jitters. The fear of second-marriage failure often prompts people to stay at arm's length relationally from one another. If the relationship intensifies, one or the other will push the destruct button labeled FEAR.

The longer a person remains single after a divorce, the greater the fear of a second marriage can become. In many people there is also the fear of losing their singleness once they have reestablished it and lived in it for some years. Thinking and caring for one person can be a lot less burdensome than thinking and caring for two people.

Where there are potential children in a second marriage, that fear can become a lot stronger. Between five and ten years of single-againness, many people have numerous relationships that end just short of marriage, while other people may ignore any relationships that could potentially lead to marriage. We all have a need to be needed by others, but some people feel safer to be needed at a distance rather than up close.

6. *Panic.* When panic strikes, rationale vanishes. In college, we had a dreaded disease called the Senior Panic. The disease was only contracted by senior girls who were not engaged by Easter of their graduating year. Pressure by parents and friends usually sent them in hot pursuit of a lifetime commitment prior to commencement. I'm sure that many of those panic choices ended in divorce.

Many single-again people admit to having gone through their own private panic in the after-divorce years, when they felt they just had to find someone special for their life before the weekend was over. About that time, the only qualification for a prospective lifetime partner had been reduced to "good credit rating." Some during that panic time make the mistake of marrying, only to be back on the sidewalk in a few short months or years.

We all panic at different times and things. It is a natural human reaction to the fear buildup. The bigger the obstacle, the greater the panic. Sometimes we call it the "What if" syndrome. "What if's" stacked end-to-end make big mountains that are hard to climb.

A good panic question to ask yourself is "Are things really as bad as they appear?" Then bounce the same question off your best friend. Then go to a good movie!

7. *Openness.* This is an honest desire to see what lies over the next mountain. Openness can say "It's okay if..." and "It's okay if not..." Openness is my availability to new experiences.

Much has been written about the Single Experience and How to Live It and Enjoy It. When it's all read and reread, you still have to hammer out your own life a day at a time. There really are no magic formulas or mystic secrets. We learn by our experiences and the shared journeys of those around us.

Experiencing openness is usually more of a process than a program. The more you discover about yourself, who you are and what you are, the more readily you will open your life to both yourself and those around you. Many of the single persons I meet around the country have gone through a divorce. They have struggled through some of the different stages we have listed here. Their lives have taken on a fresh new perspective about living. They have chosen not to blame their past for their present. They have gently put their yesterdays to rest. Their cause is not singleness and their cure is not singleness. They are not defending it or denying it. They are building on it.

There are four very positive yardsticks you can measure your growth by as you count the years since divorce.

1. Are you still stuck? Are you still where you were several years back? Have you grown but find yourself stuck right now?

2. Are you growing? Are enough new changes taking place in your life to cause you to grow? Are you being "stretched"? Are you too comfortable where you are?

3. Are you healing? It can take a lifetime to heal some hurts. Are you free enough to allow the accumulated hurts of your yesterdays to find healing strength in your todays?

4. Are you willing to be a becomer? That is simply a person caught in the process of becoming what God wants you to be. Some people never know because they are afraid to ask, "What do you want me to be, Lord?"

The Balanced Life After Divorce

To many divorced people, the term "balanced life" means to get married again, and in so doing get back in balance. If that were true, to be unmarried would mean to forever be out of balance. The truth is that a person can be married and out of balance or single and out of balance. A person can also be married and in balance or single and in balance.

Scripture sets a guideline for balanced living for all of us in Luke 2:52: "And Jesus increased in wisdom and stature, and in favor with God and men."

Jesus, although the Son of God, had to keep His life in balance in His earthly journey. To do this meant He had to find a balance between the mental, the social, the physical, and the spiritual. The emphasis was not 90 percent spiritual with the leftovers going to mental, social, and physical. For Jesus it had to be balanced. For you and for me it has to be in balance. What do these four areas mean?

1. *Mental.* God gives us a mind to use. He expects it to be stretched, sharpened, and honed. He intends to have us *think* with it. Wisdom comes from God through the function of our mind.

2. *Social.* God created us as social beings. He even gave a companion to Adam to illustrate this. We have a need to belong. We have a need to experience community and friendships. Even Jesus had this need as He built His circles of relationships on earth.

3. *Physical.* The Bible teaches that our body is a temple and that we glorify God through the proper care and use of it. We have a responsibility to properly maintain this great gift of God.

4. *Spiritual.* Jesus grew through the sharing of His life with other people in communication, healing, prayer, and love. Balanced living is growing in our relationship with God. It's a daily thing, a part of our journey.

There is a life to be lived after divorce. Some people choose to die along with their divorce. Some choose to go out into orbit in their own universe after divorce. Others choose to get lost in divorce country. Still others choose to live, grow, and rebuild. And another few just survive from year to year. What about you? The discussion questions may help you rethink where you are and where you are headed. Remember the saying, "If you don't know who you are, you may not know where you are going!"

To Think About...

1. Of the seven stages listed in this chapter, share which one you feel you are currently in.

2. Which one was the toughest for you, and why?

3. Share with your group a stage you may have gone through that is not listed.

4. Share one or two things you have learned to do in your postdivorce years that you did not do when you were married.

5. In the area of living the balanced life, which area do you struggle the most with, and why?

Chapter 2

Adjusting
Your Focus

I have always looked with envy on camera buffs. They usually tote around a camera bag full of gadgets on their shoulder and a camera with a ten-foot lens dangling around their neck. They seem to be constantly adjusting their camera and shooting pictures of everything around them. They know what kind of film to buy, what kind of filter to use, and what lens adjustment to make in order to get perfect pictures. I marvel at their knowledge and also at the finished product.

I like the cameras that do it all for you—just aim and shoot. Even then, my finished product is a few levels below that of the proverbial weekend photographer. My film friends tell me the secret to taking good pictures is in how you line up your subject and in how you focus your lens.

I think the way we view life depends on how we adjust our focus. I meet many people who either disdain the single life or constantly extol its virtues. Perhaps the happy balance for the postdivorce single person is making an adjustment somewhere between the two.

My friend Jean Hughes, a longtime single-again person, feels there are six or seven primary focus areas that she and many of her friends have gone through. Most of them seem to be a natural progression in living beyond divorce.

The first area begins when a person turns the entire focus of life on himself. Some have suggested this as the basic need to survive in the heat of a crisis. The divorce attack is often directional: All the arrows appear to be headed in the same direction—at your head. Self-focus can be self-protection at this stage of the game. The inner question is often, "Can I live through this?" If a "Yes" answer comes back, it is usually followed by a second question: "How?" The danger of self-focus is that it can eventually become a way of life.

We have all met a few selfish people in life. Have you ever wondered how they got that way? Adjusting your focus at this time of your life means doing what you need to do for yourself but not allowing a survival lifestyle to ultimately become a self-centered lifestyle. Having a community of good solid friends at this time will help you keep balanced. I am always amazed when people in divorce recovery seminars start listening to the struggles of other people. I find they start adjusting their focus from themselves to the needs and struggles of others. They become persons for others.

The emotions of confusion, panic, hurt, and depression are so very personal that we often wrap ourselves up in them. The tighter our wrapping, the more difficult it is to release the self-focus. Inner things tend to be more personal than outer things. It is more difficult to share them and work for their resolution.

I encourage the self-focusing person to find some areas

in his life where he can focus on other people. You have to get out of yourself if you are to be a growing person. Someone has said that a person wrapped up in himself makes a very small package.

A second area that many people fall into is focusing on nothing and no one, not even themselves. These are people who seem to live in the perennial fog of nondirection. They have a tendency to wait for those around them to make their life happen. They wander in and out of singles' groups, often taking without giving. They show little interest in who the people around them are. Some in this area focus on using other people. Sexual exploitation, emotional exploitation, and financial exploitation are some of the more common ways. No focus means no definite objective. No definite objective means no direction.

The nonfocusing person often specializes in the denying of reality: Reality is replaced by fantasy. We all have our momentary lapses into fantasy, but we can seldom escape reality for very long. The question that needs to be asked with frequency is the same question that the rabbit asked the skin horse in that great satirical book *The Velveteen Rabbit*: "What is real?"

Reality is rebuilding your world, not looking for a new one that is already built. It is sorting out the pieces of the puzzle of your life, then putting them back in place to make a discernible picture.

The third area of focus involves centering in on that "special someone" in your life. After the debris of divorce has been somewhat cleared from the landscape of your life, thoughts of building a new and possibly permanent relationship form. This ties into an area mentioned in another chapter—the fear syndrome. The primary fear here is the fear of getting hurt emotionally by another person if the relationship does not end in marriage.

Some of my single-again friends have said that only a fool keeps risking getting hurt in a relationship. They may be right, but a person who quits risking quits living. Many men and women will only date the same person once or twice, then move on to others. This becomes their safeguard to deepening involvements. It also can become a wall to hide behind.

I have watched numerous new relationships being formed in my work with single-again persons. Many of these have culminated in marriages that I have had the privilege to perform. Many of those marriages continue to grow as the years pass. I believe firmly in remarriage and the happiness it can bring to many lives. But there are some cautions I have learned from observing and interacting in these relationships.

1. *Give them time to develop.* When you think of remarriage later in life, be aware that you are tying two long histories together. You have to hear them, understand them, and assimilate them. That seldom happens in a 30-day romance. Too many single-again people want to make up for lost time. Hasty marriages have a high fallout rate.

2. *Don't drop all your friends when you start focusing on that special someone.* It is a natural thing to want to be with the person you care about, but your friends need to be a part of your journey too. I have watched too many singles corral a live prospect and vanish from their support system only to reappear weeks or months later when the relationship fails. Your friends can help you be honest with yourself as they affirm and support your new relationship.

3. *That special someone usually has a family.* Someone has said that the blended family normally comes with carrying charges. For younger people remarrying after a divorce, it means that you might have the children of both spouses now living under one roof. There are numerous books that have been written on this topic. For older singles, the other family is still there; they just won't be living under your roof. It takes time to meet them, know them, understand them, and even like them a little.

Sometimes old feelings come with new relatives. It will take a while to understand those feelings. Feelings are rooted in history. Each of us has one!

4. *Talk, talk, talk!* One of the top ten reasons for marriage failure over the past 20 years has been lack of communication. There are two kinds of communication, both before and after marriage. Maintenance talk is one and heart-soul talk is the other.

Maintenance talk is simply talking about all the essential (and sometimes nonessential) things of our life. It is routine talk. It is easy conversation. It consists of everything and nothing. It takes care of the business of living on a daily basis. We can't live without it, but it can't be the only thing we live with.

Heart-soul talk is reaching down deep inside ourselves and talking about feelings, dreams, hopes, fears, struggles, and desires. It seldom comes easily because it puts us in a position of vulnerability. It yanks the safe maintenance mask from our being and exposes the raw nerves of our life. Heart-soul talk keeps us in touch with each other in a vital relationship. It is fairly easy to live on the surface communicatively, but it is hard work to probe beneath the surface. Heart-soul talk means lots of listening as well as talking.

There is a decided adjustment when you go from just focusing on yourself or focusing on no one to focusing on someone special. It is a time when both a settling calm and a nervous anxiety seem to battle for center stage in your life. The oft-used term "second adolescence" might be the most descriptive. Some will run toward it while others will run from it.

The fourth area of focus appears when the single-again person becomes bored or burned out on the single life. He has a desire to settle down, but the focus is not necessarily on "the" special someone but on "any" special someone. Selectivity is replaced by convenience. Many first-time marriages were marriages of convenience. Too many second marriages fall into the same category.

The feeling comes from being worn out in searching. The longer one has remained single, the lower the acceptance level can fall. The fear of growing old alone can reduce the compatibility margin. The list of things longed for in a relationship gets pared to an acceptable minimum. Genuine love can easily be traded for comfortable security attached to a live body (sometimes a semilive body).

Many people have shared the "tired of looking" complex with me and have changed their sign to read "no reasonable offer refused." The real question is, "What kind of lasting relationship will this kind of exchange produce?" The danger is in creating a somewhat boring marriage where the participants are merely serving a sentence rather than building a dynamic relationship.

Some single-again persons consider this kind of relationship a fair trade-off. It could be considered a mere adjustment in focus or it could be living the rest of one's life out of focus.

A fifth area is closely akin to the last one. It involves relationships that reach the level of companionship but never reach the doorway of marriage. Many people have three-, four-, or five-year relationships with one person. Usually only one person in the relationship is mentally altar-bound. The other puts off any attempt in that direction. One holds on for marriage while the other holds on for companionship. Few of these relationships ever culminate in marriage. They usually end up with an emotional divorce.

Some single-again people in this group want the best of two worlds: They want the feeling of being special to someone and of having someone special to them, but they also want to retain their freedom as a single person. Men sometimes fall into this category. A few have told me that they want the serious relationship and the companionship it affords but do not want the emotional and economic responsibility. That's almost like saying, "I want a new car and all it affords, but I want to make the payments when I feel like it, not when the bank tells me." Commitment always brings responsibility. Responsibility brings accountability.

Past memories seem to come in like a flood when new relationships are progressing. The renewed feeling of past hurts waves many caution flags. This causes many people to keep relationships at arm's length.

Career goals can keep the companionship relationship on hold. Some people are afraid of what they will lose, while others fear what they might gain.

Too few singles in the companionship spectrum really evaluate where their relationship is headed. Days, weeks, months, even years can pass without honest appraisal of the situation. If both parties want and are receiving the same thing, that's fine. But in too many cases the signals are very mixed and the disappointments loom larger as time passes.

Sometimes in counseling, as I listen to someone share a situation with me, I have only one question to ask: "Is this situation healthy for you on an ongoing basis?" If you can live with it and grow with it, fine. If not, you may need to take action on it.

The sixth area of focus is accepting the fact that a marriage or remarriage can add to a person's life without robbing him of his identity. I have listened to hundreds, probably thousands of single-again persons tell me how they fought to find their identity that they had lost or submerged within their marriage. Their greatest fear is to lose that identity in another marriage. And their fear is justified. There are still numerous people out there who are looking for someone to take over and direct in life. What better place to do it legally than in marriage? they reason.

I have watched nice, quiet, "go along" persons change overnight once they marry. Their need to dominate and direct, and control takes over where the wedding recessional ends.

For many divorced persons, the battle to regain self-esteem and self-worth is a long one. Both men and women struggle with it. As a person discovers his identity, his values and priorities are often realigned. As he becomes aware of them, he desires to share them with people who have gone through the same struggle. Once you know the freedom of winning a struggle, you want to retain it. You also want other people to retain theirs.

Healthy persons are not identity-robbers. They are identity-*givers*. My experience has taught me that some of the best candidates for remarriage fall into this category. They have climbed the same mountain.

Some of you are asking, "Where are all the people in this category?" Many of them are standing close by. They usually are very recognizable by the quiet confidence they exude. They aren't the noisemakers in the singles world. They are the bridgebuilders!

The last area of focus deals with how we focus on God and how we allow Him to focus on us. We often view each other through distorted lenses in life. We too often look at what we can *get* from another person rather than what we can *give* to another person. People get out of focus for us, and we get out of focus for them. I believe that God is our catalyst in the focusing process.

A key to this is found in John 10:10, where Jesus said, "I have come that they might have life, and that they may have it more abundantly." Jesus makes clear the reason why He came: He came to introduce life—not just plain vanilla life but life in abundant quantities. Hot fudge sundae life. Real life.

Some single-again persons feel that this kind of life is reserved for married people only. Jesus made no distinctions between single and married. His only distinction was in the quality and enormity of the life He brought. He offered it to any and all takers.

I have met single people who not only have each other out of focus but also have God out of focus. I have met still others who focus better on the people in their life because they view them through the eyes and lens of God. They don't use and abuse people for their own ends. They are wide open to the people whom God will bring into their life when they are ready. They will fine-tune on each one and seek God's direction in allowing that relationship to grow. They refuse to stay focused on themselves. And they don't focus on other people merely so that their own needs will be met.

These singles don't operate from the despair side of life. They are neither burned out nor bored out. The identity they have discovered for themselves is tied to what they have discovered about God.

Earlier in this chapter we said that some people have to work their way through all of these areas as they adjust their focus on the people who populate their lives in special ways. Some of you will use the list to identify where you are right now, and will hope you can avoid the next step in the order. Others will see where they have been and celebrate where they are. There are always some in-between steps, stages, and places that we have not covered. No list is a ladder that must have every rung stepped upon. We have tried to hit some key ones that people have said they experienced.

The important thing is to always ask the question, "Do I really have this in focus?" Life is not a Shure-Shot camera. It is a series of adjustments and focusing. We learn from other people and allow them to learn from us. Where are you in your focusing?

To Think About . . .

1. In this chapter we listed seven areas of focus on post-

divorce living. Which one best describes your current existence?

2. Share what you have learned and experienced in passing through some of these areas.

3. What are the things that get you "out of focus" in living beyond divorce?

4. Share with your group some of the things you have learned in building postdivorce relationships.

5. Finish this statement: "Getting my life in better focus means _____."

Chapter 3

The Healing Process

Hurts caused by the divorce experience are seldom healed overnight. Because we live in a world dominated by the "instant," we have a difficult time believing that everything does not fall into this pattern. One of those noninstant things is the healing process.

The tangible things relating to a divorce experience can be managed, directed, filed, and resolved in a few short years. The intangible often takes many years to resolve.

I have personally talked with many people who are six, eight, and ten years beyond their divorce but still wrestle with the open wounds of divorce in their heart. For many reasons they do not seek a resolution to the hurts through the healing process. Living without experiencing healing will permanently stunt your growth.

There are several major wounds that a divorce inflicts upon a person. The first involves *pride*. Divorce is the failure of a relationship. When we fail at something, we look bad. Our pride in ourselves and our abilities is questioned and scarred. We can get angry at ourselves and we can get angry at the person wounding our pride. Divorce wars are usually fought on the subjective and the objective level. The blame bounces back and forth like a Ping-Pong ball. Too many people never find the healing for their crumpled pride. The climb back to wholeness becomes a series of detours through the world of singleness.

A second wound involves *vengeance*. Vengeance says, "You hurt me and you deserve to be hurt back." I have watched unresolved vengeance matches go on for years after a divorce. It becomes a hobby, a weekend sport. Vengeance is stirred up when we have been wronged. For many people the wrong is only solved by reprisal.

Our judicial system in divorce litigation is often referred to as the adversary system. Our system seems to cheer on the vengeance contest. During the legal processing of a divorce, most who have been there know the intensity of this stress.

I sometimes share Romans 12:19 with people who appear caught in the vortex of vengeance. The verse says, "Beloved, do not avenge yourselves, but rather give place to wrath; for it is written, 'Vengeance is mine, I will repay,' says the Lord." The problem with most people who hear this is that they want to know *when* God will repay. Apparently they want to buy tickets for the event and cheer the repayment!

When vengeance is turned over to God, a healing release begins to take place in your life. When dealt with humanly, there is no end to getting enough vengeance. When given to God, we are set free to start experiencing God's healing.

A third wound that is often opened up is *hopelessness*.

Solving the divorce dilemma is one thing, and most people attain it. Looking toward the future with the past always in instant replay in your mind can cause a sense of daily hopelessness. I meet many long-divorced singles who appear to be possessed with a hopeless spirit. They say things like, "It isn't fair." "My years are all wasted." "I am condemned to singleness forever." They act, look, think, and live the word *hopeless*.

Healing a hopeless spirit involves allowing God to bring His hope into your life and realizing that the apostle Paul's words to the Roman Christians were words of healing: "And we know that all things work together for good to those who love God, to those who are the called according to His purpose" (Romans 8:28).

We are all daily participants in the healing process. Living is the constant resolution of hurtful experiences. We are both the hurting and the healed as we make our daily journey through life. There are five major areas in the beyond-divorce years that can be looked at through the healing perspective.

The Healing of Memories

Life is the making of a memory. Each day is a page of memories, both good and bad, in our book of life. We often have a tendency to magnify the bad ones and minimize the good ones. We cry much over bad ones and celebrate too little the good ones. The news media specialize in the bad stuff and often leave a good story until the closing minutes.

The difference between the death of a mate and the divorce of a mate is that death leaves you with a file of good memories of yesterday while divorce leaves you with a "ring-around-the-collar" memory of yesterday. Any good memories prior to divorce tend to be long forgotten after the divorce.

Some people seem to deal with these memories by

denying that they ever existed. They appear able to totally block them from their mind. Whether good or bad, they dismiss both. They forget that you file the good and learn from the bad. Denial only equips us to perfect the art more each day we live. Denial can become a living death.

Other people collect memories and treasure them. They become the family albums of the mind. They were lived out and are now part of the collectibles of our lives. They are spoken of freely, both the good and the bad. They are accepted as the landscape of our life.

What do you do with the memories that are painful to you? The ones that caused deep hurt? The ones you try to file but the file drawer keeps opening up and dumping the contents back on your life? I believe that hurtful memories from yesterday and today have to be prayerfully given over to God for ultimate resolution and filing. That prayer often starts with the words, "Lord, I feel..." It is asking God to take the feelings, unscramble them, resolve them, and give us His peace concerning them. It means that we also ask God to take care of not only past painful memories but also our present hurts and our fears of future hurts. God has many ways of healing our memories. He simply waits for us to ask so that He can begin the process.

I occasionally meet people who refuse to have memories healed. They want to keep them alive so that the pain they cause will keep them living on the defensive. They feel that this will protect them from further hurts. Underneath all this can lie a basic unresolved anger that can affect or infect a life for years to come.

Healing a memory is letting it go. It is not holding on to it. Unhealed memories can make for a heavy load as we travel through life. The unhealed memories of yesterday are giant roadblocks in the road to tomorrow.

Memories that need healing are often hurts of the heart. They are hard to deal with and own because they lie deep within us. They are difficult to verbalize. Sometimes writing these hurts out on paper helps put them into a visible context. They are collections of thoughts, past spoken words, human treatment, feelings—all tightly wound and stored within our heart. They are not easy to dislodge. When there are too many that go unresolved, hearts become broken! Turning them over to God is a long process, but well worth the processing.

A very helpful little chart that can help you enact that process appears in the book by the Linn Brothers, *Healing Life's Hurts*. In the healing of a memory, the authors state that there are five progressive stages that a person can go through.

1. I don't admit I was ever hurt: *Denial*
2. I blame others for hurting and destroying me: *Anger*
3. I set up conditions to be fulfilled before I'm ready to forgive: *Bargaining*
4. I blame myself for letting hurt destroy me: *Depression*
5. I look forward to growth from hurt: *Acceptance*

Think about this a little and see where you are in the healing of your memories.

Healing Through Forgiveness

For many people the most difficult chapter in my early book, *Growing Through Divorce*, dealt with forgiveness. Most early reactions were expressed by the comments, "I didn't need that chapter" and "That's impossible!" Since those early responses, I have collected a file of letters and personal accounts of the dramatic changes that took place in people's lives when they sought to practice the principles we shared. In brief those principles are: I ask God to forgive me for my divorce; I forgive myself; I ask my ex-spouse to forgive me; I receive their forgiveness. When practiced, these do not guarantee the restoration of a marital relationship, although that has happened.

However, these do bring about a total cleansing process that allows a person to *live forgiven*.

I have discovered that forgiveness is not a one-time thing. It is something that you and I need to practice all through our lives. Many divorced people employed the five principles above and were renewed in the process. Then they forgot its importance in their daily lives and continued to live around it rather than in it. Many have said that the one great thing they gained from their divorce was really learning to deal with forgiveness for the first time.

One of the best biblical examples of forgiveness and how it works is found in Genesis chapters 37 through 45.

Joseph was sold into slavery in Egypt by his brothers. Even though this distress sent his life in a totally new and unwanted direction, he clearly forgave his brothers, and in so doing he was able to release any pent-up bitterness he felt.

Years later in Egypt, when his brothers came to buy grain, Joseph wept when he saw his brothers. Because forgiveness was already processed, he did not seek vengeance. Weeping can bring an emotional release that sets us free to experience another phase of enacted forgiveness. Joseph's earlier experience had to be a painful one, but God helped him accept it in line with His purpose for his life. God even took care of the healing of the bad memory of Joseph's encounter with Potiphar's wife.

Joseph's eventual imprisonment did not seem to sway him from God's direction and purpose for his life. His forgiveness was based on his knowledge that the Lord was with him. If forgiveness would not have been God's healing stream running through Joseph's life, he might have died in prison or never escaped the bottom of the well. How do you measure up to Joseph in the forgiveness category? His total forgiveness of his brothers brought about a greater friendship in the end of his life than he had with them at the beginning. Forgiveness is always a *process*; you learn about it by practicing it!

Solitary Healing

Some parts of our healing process can take place only in solitary confinement. That doesn't mean we spend a year in isolation in a cabin in the desert or mountains. It *does* mean that a vital part of the healing of hurts in our lives needs to take place when we are alone.

I believe that the longer you and I live in a noisy, overcrowded world, the more we will need the discipline of solitude in our lives. Two key things can happen in our times of solitude. First, we can get back in touch with ourselves. Reflecting, thinking, sorting out our feelings can only be done well in places of solitude. We are so used to turning on knobs that fill our lives with noise that it takes strong discipline to just sit quietly and think. So many of our strings are pulled by other people that only the frayed ends are left for us to grasp at the end of a week. We have to establish a center for ourselves where we can rediscover who we really are.

The second quality of solitude is in using it to get in touch with God. Scripture tells us, "Be still and know that I am God" (Psalm 46:10). Many of us talk to God, but too few of us listen to God. Many great biblical characters refused to move a muscle until God talked to them. We are too used to moving on our own and hoping that God will sanction the move somewhere along the line. Study, prayer, meditation, and praise begin best in solitude before they move in a community forum.

Solitary healing is allowing God's quietness, assurance, and peace to wash over me with a healing effect. This does not come easily; it takes long hours of discipline and work. An increasingly popular way to begin this process is by taking a two-day retreat for yourself in the quiet of a monastery or retreat center. Many of the best ones around the country are Catholic. Morning and evening there is the opportunity for corporate worship while the in-between times are given to your own study, prayer, and growth. When most of us think of a retreat, we think of spending a weekend with a hundred other people at a Christian conference center. This is a retreat, but certainly not one of solitude. We need both kinds.

Some of God's best healing of life's hurts comes when we are one-to-one with God. It is not the easiest kind but often the most needed kind.

Healing in Community

When you think about healing in community, you might think about a hospital. It is a collection of people desiring healing all under the same roof but with different illnesses and different treatments. If the treatment is successful, you leave the hospital and stay far away as long as you can.

Your church or your group of friends should be a healing community for you. Unlike the hospital, you don't leave them when you receive healing. You stay to celebrate your healing and to help others heal their hurts.

In his book *The Wounded Healer*, Henri Nouwen says, "A Christian community is therefore a healing community not because wounds are cured and pains are alleviated, but because wounds and pains become openings or occasions for a new vision. Mutual confession then becomes a mutual deepening of hope, and sharing weakness becomes a reminder to one and all of the coming strength."

In a sense we are all wounded healers. But as our wounds are healed we become more equipped to be healers to others.

I am amazed at the kind of help that people in divorce recovery workshops can give to each other. They all come the first night concentrating on their own wounds and bringing about their own healing. By the third night they have often shifted the focus of looking at their own wounds to looking at the wounds of others and how they might become healers to those people. As they bring healing, they become whole.

I have always felt that a good, healthy singles' group should offer two things to all who come through the door: healing and wholeness. I am not intimating that all who come through the door are sick. I am saying that all should have the opportunity for any healing and wholeness that they might need in their life.

After you have been around a singles' group for a long time, there is a danger that you will burn out on the group. That appears to happen to those who don't have a healthy balance between giving and receiving. The more you receive, the more you have to give. The more you give, the more you will receive. That's really a biblical pattern referred to many times in the New Testament.

Medical science has discovered that those who can help ailing people best are those who have had or have the same illness. The "me too" often brings the brightest ray of hope to the hurting. Solitude and community: They seem to be direct opposites in helping heal hurts, but they are really companions.

Healing in Family Relationships

Living beyond divorce means living with families. Divorce helps you gain relatives and lose relatives. It amplifies misunderstandings and isolates people. It causes the question "Where did we go wrong?" to remain unanswered by most parents. Divorce doesn't affect just the immediate family in a divorce; it affects the extended family of parents, grandparents, aunts, uncles, cousins, nephews, and nieces. It erects barriers where once there were bridges. It silences voices that once were treasured.

It often takes many years postdivorce to bring healing to ruptured relationships. To be isolated from one's parents because of a divorce and the sides that were taken is a lonely and cruel thing. To lose in-laws that you were close to leaves a tremendous void in a life. Inheriting a new family by a new marriage somehow doesn't always remove the sting of losing treasured people from your life.

There is no easy street to travel in bringing healing to relatives after a divorce. You may want things to be as they once were, but others are often not as willing.

I have watched people living beyond divorce in desperate loneliness because they have been cut off from family because of judgments and misunderstandings. Is the restoration possible? Can things be again as they once were on the other side of divorce? Probably not. But genuine efforts can be made to bring a healing touch to the situations.

A first suggestion is always to pray about renewal of lost relationships. A second is to be unafraid to go to those relatives and ask for their friendship. Sometimes you discover that both want the same thing but both are afraid to make their feelings known. Silence only deepens the chasm of separation. A third suggestion is to allow friends to help rebuild the broken relationship. They can often be the healer for you in your situation.

It is a horrible waste to live a lifetime postdivorce and be robbed of family relationships that can enrich your own journey. Has your divorce long robbed you of some people you need around you? If it has, make a list and go to work on the healing of family relationships.

To Think About...

1. Of the three wounds from a divorce—pride, vengeance,

and hopelessness—which has been the toughest for you to experience healing in?

2. What memory of your divorce seems to remain unhealed after all these years?

3. What happened to you when you experienced the forgiveness process in your divorce?

4. How do you feel about the solitary healing process?

5. Has your "community" been a healing agent for you? How?

Chapter 4

The Uncomfortable Crown

Every September I join millions of Americans in watching the Miss America Pageant. Along with Labor Day, it marks the end of summer. It is about as traditional as a Fourth of July picnic. If you don't watch it, you have to find out who won it.

Every time I watch it, I am amazed that a situation that takes place in the closing minutes is never resolved. As the Miss America for the new year walks down the runway, her crown usually teeters and totters and appears ready to fall off at any minute. A few winners of the past have had to steady it with their free hand. I am amazed that a production of this size and enormity cannot find a simple way to keep a crown from slipping. Perhaps the slipping crown is symbolic of the glory of the moment.

It starts slipping the minute you receive it and has slipped all the way off by the end of the year, when the reign expires.

Crowns are like that. With all their honor and pomp and glory, they slip a little so that they won't be taken too seriously.

Each of us contends with the crown problem. Many postdivorce, single-again people resent having to exchange the marriage crown for the single crown. It doesn't seem quite fair. You work hard during your late teenage years to get rid of your single crown. You finally trade it in for the marital crown, and some years down the road you are swapping it again for the single crown. For many people the problem with the single crown is the lettering upon it. Its imprimatur is often F-A-I-L-U-R-E. Who wants to wear that in public?

There are three kinds of crowns that a single-again person can choose to wear. The first is the kind of crown that those around you want to place on your head. It can be stamped with two different words: *Failure* or *Success*.

The Crown of Success

Prestige, fame, recognition, achievement. Our society is a society of acclamation. We reward with a crown those who climb the rocky road to success. It may be in the form of an oscar, an Emmy, a gold watch, a promotion, applause, a hot fudge sundae, or a congratulations card. In our world, the road to success is sometimes called "upward mobility." The only problem with this is that the higher you climb the tree of success, the less branches there are to support you!

The crown of success brings with it power. Power means control. Control means that I can tell other people what to do while I myself do as I please.

Most of us have watched those who have climbed to the top and gained their crown, only to lose it and fall back down to the bottom. Our response can be that they never deserved it anyway, or else a sadness that they simply did not know how to deal with it.

Wearing the crown of success is a cautious problem. It is learning not to take yourself too seriously. It is a gentle acceptance without an ego distortment. There is nothing wrong with success if you can handle it properly. The handmaiden to success is always responsibility. Scripture teaches the principle "To whom much has been committed, of him they will ask the more" (Luke 12:48).

The world is in the business of handing out crowns. The danger is that they become quickly tarnished, often cumbersome, and soon forgotten.

Many single-again people fall into the trap of crown-collecting. They feverishly look for an assortment of crowns to replace the ones they have lost. They might want to say, "Hey, look at me. I'm not so bad." We all need acceptance and affirmation; the key is in how we attain it and wear it.

The Crown of Failure

More crowns of failure are passed out each day than crowns of success. Some are self-imposed while many are imposed by other people. Divorce is the failure of a relationship between two people. Does this mean that the people who were a part of that relationship are now called failures?

The word "failure" seems to hit a person on three fronts. The first is the *feeling level*. The second is the *acceptance level* and the third is the *recovery level*.

We all know the feeling of failure. It is as much a part of our daily journey as the newspaper. We have some days to which we want to tie a "failure knot"— and permanently forget. At the end of those days we have to separate the acts of failure from the person. If we don't, we will easily be lost in the failure syndrome, and our favorite words will be "I can't!"

One of the most helpful things I have discovered in my own life is that I have the freedom to fail. This doesn't mean that I plan to self-destruct the things I attempt to do. It *does* mean that I have the freedom to succeed and the freedom to fail. Believe me, I would rather succeed! But I cannot let a failure be a deterrent to continuing to try. Perhaps this is why I believe so strongly in second marriages. Being nailed to the failure of your first one for the rest of your life can quickly make you believe that *you* are a failure. I'm glad that God's love package includes forgiveness.

Feelings of the fear of repeated failure not only keep people from a second marriage but also keep them from attempting things that will help them grow and become a fulfilled person. The thread of success is finely woven between failure and trying again!

Acceptance of failure is fully recognizing what transpired and attempting to learn something from it. It is learning to say out loud, "I blew it!" Ego and self-preservation often bar the door to confession. We set ourselves up to be believable and flawless. When we have to admit we are not, it's a bad day at Black Rock. Again, accepting a failure and taking responsibility for it does not mean that *you* are a failure.

Recovery time from a failure can depend upon whether it was tiny or gigantic. A marriage failure usually falls into the gigantic category because it affects so many people. The more players on the stage, the longer the recovery process. Not all recover at the same pace. I believe in recovery more than adjustment. Adjustment can mean I never quite get to where I want to be. I just rearrange the pieces of the puzzle from time to time and keep on breathing. Recovery says I am over it and finished with it!

The crown of failure often carries with it intense pain. It is easy to say that there is no growth without pain. If we had our choice, many of us would be *short* on the growing end. Few of us embrace pain. We do everything in our power to avoid it. We consume vitamins, pills, potions—anything that will prevent pain.

Honest pain must be felt, experienced, and walked through. It cannot be escaped if we are to learn and grow from it. Just make sure your pain is not self-inflicted. It needs to come from an honest source in order to produce growth. Self-inflicted pain leads to self-pity, and self-pity usually leads to depression. And depression is the pits!

Yes, the world passes out its crowns. For some people the crown can become a brand. For others it can be a graduation sign of new growth.

A second kind of crown is the kind you give yourself. Self-imposed crowns are dangerous. They run the extreme from "I'm the Greatest" to "I'm the Worst." They range from ego-centered to egoless. They deal with self-importance to nonimportance. They cause us to sit on pedestals or fall into the cracks in the sidewalk.

Situations that we experience in life define how we will crown ourself. Self-worth is a problem for many single-again people. I meet many singles in my travels who spend all their time staring at their shoes. They are down because of their situation and they keep looking down to enforce the situation. If I tell them that they are *God's unique, unrepeatable miracle*, they just keep staring at their shoes as they shuffle off. A divorce, though long ago history, often dictates their present-day worth. Their crown says *NOT WORTH MUCH*.

Alienation is another self-imposed crown. When self-worth is low, our worth to other people is even lower. It is easy at this point to become a hibernation specialist. Four walls are easier to deal with than four people. Many single-again people cut themselves off from singles communities with the excuse that they are bored by it all. Perhaps the real reason is that they are not in touch with themselves and therefore cannot be significantly in touch with other people. Alienation promotes the "poor me" syndrome. It locks a person into his own cocoon.

A cure for alienation is to reach out and touch someone. It is a tough process to get used to once you have locked yourself away. But it won't take long to enjoy once you knock your walls down.

A third self-imposed crown is stamped *NONPRODUC-TIVE*. One of my goals in helping people through the journey after divorce is to help them develop and set goals. It is easy to live both goalless and on a contingency basis as a single-again person. You can even wait for a special someone to come your direction with a briefcase full of goals that you can readily adapt to your life. I meet many "waiters" around the country. They have chosen to remain nonproductive until someone makes them productive or until they feel they have a reason to be productive.

In the first five years after a divorce most people feel they will soon remarry, so they choose to live on a somewhat tentative basis. Career changes, academic pursuits, and geographical changes all go on hold. You never know who you will meet and what plans they will already have forged. After ten years of being single again and living this way, it's easy to get upset with a tentative lifestyle. A sense of permanence does not always come in the form of other people; we have to create our own by assuming direction for our life. If you are feeling the crown of nonproductivity slipping down around your throat, whose responsibility is it to remove it? Yours! Moving ahead depends on *you*. As someone has said, "If you don't know where you are going, how will you know when you have arrived there?"

There are numerous other invisible crowns that single-again people wear. They are as prolific as badges at a convention. They are stamped with the words *ONGOING GUILT, CONSTANT REJECTION, LONELINESS AND MORE LONELINESS, SINGLE IS A SENTENCE* and in small print *Deliver Me!*

Have you placed some self-imposed crowns on your life

that don't really belong there? If you have, identify them and free yourself from them. Unwanted crowns have a way of choking the life out of you!

We have talked about two kinds of crowns to this point—the kind that other people give you and the kind you give yourself. Both kinds have some good points to them and some bad points. Some are liabilities and some are assets. All are daily arrayed on the mantle of life.

The God-Given Crown

There is a third kind of crown I want to talk about. It can replace some of the unwanted crowns if you will allow it to. It is the kind of crown that God gives us. I know, you are already singing the old spiritual, "I've got a crown, you've got a crown, all God's chillun got a crown." But no. This is a different kind of crown.

In James 1:12 we read these words: "Blessed is the man who endures temptation, for when he has been proved, he will receive the crown of life, which the Lord has promised to those who love Him." Some of you are whipping out your calculator to add up your trials as you get ready to dash out and collect your crown. But you will have to delay delivery on your crown for now. I doubt that all your trials are over. This verse really tells us that God has a crown that falls into a different category from the world's. It is a crown of life that leads to real living. It is permanent and can be worn with pride. It is not people-imposed or self-imposed. It is God-imposed.

God's crown is not always visible to those around us. It is not a status symbol. It is God's seal of approval for what we have walked through and endured as His children. Too many single again-people feel that they are on God's blacklist rather than on His crown list. James says, "*Blessed* is the man." It doesn't say it excludes the divorced person. God specializes in being inclusive rather than exclusive.

Peter also writes about the kind of crown that God plans to give you. First Peter 5:4 says, "When the Chief Shepherd appears, you will receive the crown of glory that does not fade away." Two things strike me in this verse. The first is its positiveness: "You will." Nothing is left to indecision or performance; it is a promise. The second striking thing is that this crown is unfading. Its brilliance and luster will never dim. It will be on view forever. How unlike the crowns that are handed out daily in life. The sparkle on them soon fades and they become barely discernible, while God's crown just keeps on shining.

There is another aspect to the crown that God gives you and me. In order for that crown to become a reality, Jesus had to don a crown of thorns earlier in His life. John 19:1-5 speaks of it:

> So then Pilate took Jesus and scourged Him. And the soldiers twisted a crown of thorns and put it on His head, and they put on Him a purple robe. Then they said, "Hail, King of the Jews!" And they struck Him with their hands. Pilate then went out again, and said to them, "Behold, I am bringing Him out to you, that you may know that I find no fault in Him." Then Jesus came out, wearing the crown of thorns and the purple robe. And Pilate said to them, "Behold the Man!"

Jesus' crown was not a regal one. It was one of shame, rejection, and humiliation. It had to be worn, and worn publicly. It caused Him physical and mental pain. Yet He wore it proudly. It was a necessary part of His journey toward the crucifixion. It was His death and resurrection that turned the crown of thorns He wore into a crown of life for you and me.

As He stood before Pilate and the crowds, Christ was unrecognized as the King of Glory. He was more looked upon as a crazy man from Galilee who made preposterous claims to be the Son of God. It was only some days later that His claims were proven true.

The world gave its crown to Jesus much as it can give crowns to you and me: It was undeserving, but He wore it. Some of the crowns you receive are undeserving, but you often have to wear them awhile. God can change the lettering on your crown of *FAILURE* to read *LOVED*, on your crown of *GUILT* to read *FORGIVEN*, on your crown of *REJECTION* to read *ACCEPTED*. Even the words *SINGLE AGAIN* can be changed to read *SINGLE AND NEW*!

Old crowns need to be replaced with new ones. Old identities need to be replaced by new ones.

SINGLE AGAIN, SINGLE STILL need not be an uncomfortable crown!

To Think About...

1. Which of the two words, "single" or "divorced" is easiest for you to handle and why?

2. How have you recovered in your life from the feelings of failure?

3. Did you experience a time of alienation in living beyond divorce? Share with your group how you felt

and what helped you out of your isolation.

4. Do you view not remarrying after your divorce as a gain or a loss in your life? Why?

Chapter 5

The Myths of Divorce

The dictionary defines the word "myth" as "an imaginary or fictitious thing or person, something having no foundation in fact." Myths are fun to think about, to read, to wish upon. It is only when you start believing them that you run into trouble.

I have discovered a number of myths that people tend to believe in the land beyond divorce. Because these myths have no foundation in fact, they become detrimental to growth. In fact, they make growth impossible.

Myths are like rumors: They seem to come from nowhere and are passed on to other people with regularity. When they are passed around long enough, they are often accepted as fact.

There are ten predominant myths that I have listened

to in the past ten years. I want to examine them and hopefully stick a pin in them and pop them. If you have been hanging onto one of them for the past few years, look out!

Myth number one: "Divorce is the end of my world."

Life is comprised of two basic things—beginnings and endings. Beginnings are times of challenge, excitement, and speculation. They are open invitations to the future for all of us. All who embarked upon marriage have felt the optimism and the thrill of a new beginning.

Endings can be times of happiness and celebration or they can be times of great sadness and emptiness. Yesterday I stood near the finish line of the 1984 Olympic Bicycle Road Race. For the person winning the gold medal, it was a great ending to a long and hard race. For the person finishing in last place, it was the agony of defeat. Both finished, but the feelings were a world apart.

Life for all of us is a series of beginnings and endings. If we are to live, we will experience both. The secret of living right is in how we handle them. Too many people vote on our beginnings and endings. When the votes are tabulated, we decide if we were a success or failure. Then we live out the tabulation.

Divorce is the end of a relationship and the closure of a marriage. It is the end of your world as you once knew it and lived it. It is not the end of the rest of your life if you choose to live it. It is not easy to bring closure to a marriage. Sometimes it takes years to close all the doors and open new ones. The longer you are married the more difficult it can be. Many marriages today end after 25 or 30 years. That demands a lot of closure and memory-sealing.

Many people live in the world of seminostalgia. When things change or do not go in the direction they want, the "way we were" syndrome sets in and sends their minds back to yesterday. There is nothing wrong with nostalgia, but it will never rebuild yesterday. Yesterday is history and today is reality.

Beginnings are the seeds planted in endings! Too many people go into years of limbo after a divorce. I wonder if it's because they have run out of seeds and allowed someone to plant a myth that says "end of my world" in their head and heart.

The sunrise of each new day signals a new beginning. It is only when you truck yesterday's baggage into it that it becomes a continuation of a journey into endings.

Divorce brings to culmination a segment of your life. It does not end your life and close the double doors to your world. If you have been living with the myth, get your pin out!

Myth number two: "No one understands me."

Have you run out of understanding people lately? Getting understanding is really a form of getting applause and affirmation. It is having someone agree with your position and reaffirm that you are okay.

Telling and retelling divorce war stories is one way of trying to be understood in the postdivorce years. I sometimes tell people in divorce recovery seminars that they know they are growing when they quit telling their stories to everyone they meet. At the outset of a divorce it is part of the healing process. Five or ten years later, telling those same stories can mean you are stuck in your growth pattern.

The people who understand divorce and its problems the most are usually those who have gone through it or those who work with those who have gone through it. They can be empathetic, understanding, and affirming, and yet be neutral and honest.

Understanding helps relieve the guilt feeling. Guilt is the imperfections of our life taking over our life. Understanding is having someone listen to your struggles and assure you that it is no sin not to be perfect.

Assumption can be a barrier to understanding. It is easy to assume that no one will understand anything we say or do or think. No understanding attempted, no release gained.

Gaining understanding is always a risk. You might be misunderstood and buried deeper in the problem. There are mountains of misunderstanding in divorce country. They may be the biggest deterrent to your ongoing journey and growth. You have to risk the mountain-climbing!

Myth number three: "My relatives and family all hate me."

If misunderstanding lives anywhere, it is in the family structures surrounding divorce. Marriages unite, divorces divide. People have an innate ability to choose sides and cheer for their team in postdivorce country. It is easy to feel that everyone closest to you hates you.

Children have a way of throwing a divorce at you with the words, "If you really loved me, you wouldn't allow this to happen." How those words sting! They can keep coming at you for many years after a divorce. Whenever the air of relationships gets thin, the biting words can pour forth. Children have a way of divorcing one parent or the other after a divorce. They pick their team, line up their feelings, and let you know they don't like you. When you listen to that for a while, you end up hating yourself. I have seen countless divorces where the children end up hating one parent or the other. Human separation can go on for years with no relational healing. About all you can do is keep your love strong even though theirs weakens.

Parents can have a way of voting you out of the family circle after a divorce. Two things seem to promote this. The first is the feeling that the parent has failed because their son or daughter experienced a divorce. The fact that you were married 30 years doesn't seem to lessen the feeling. The second is simply personal and human embarrassment. Most normal parents of all ages want their children to make them look good as parents. The rewards of parenting are never supposed to stop. It is helpful to talk your divorce through with your parents regardless of their age. Let them know that it wasn't their fault and that you are sorry they had to live through it. Don't let the mountains of unsaid words pile up and cause a relationship gap that widens through the years.

In-laws in divorce can make you feel like an outlaw. Once-close relationships can evaporate overnight. Children can lose their grandparents, and you can be made to feel like a thief. Sometimes hatred from in-laws develops because they have never been told the facts, or if they have been told, they choose not to believe them. At other times, an ex-spouse can stack the cards against you with his or her family.

If you feel your children hate you, your parents hate you, and your in-laws hate you, you can easily absorb the injection and start hating yourself.

Votes of confidence from family members do not come easily in a divorce. Find those who love you still and let them encircle your wagon! It is a myth to believe that they all hate you.

Myth number four: "I'll never remarry."

I have listened to those three words perhaps more than any others in the past ten years. After you have listened to a divorce story for a couple of hours, it can end with those three words for a benediction. I understand the feeling that prompts them. After being hurt, who wants to subject themselves to possible further hurt ever again?

The words "I'll never remarry" are the ultimate armor of human protection. In the beginning they are said as a threat and a protection device. Five years down the road from a divorce they can be said out of despair. Ten years later they come from tired lives who have been involved in serious relationships that have not worked out. At this juncture a relational burnout sets into a person's life. Forever-singleness looks less tiring than terminal involvements. The "I'll-never-remarry" credo has gone from the defensive to the offensive to the reclusive.

By way of encouragement, let me say that I have seen people remarry in all three stages. Surprises can come in human form at any moment in your life. Perhaps they come quickest when we fight least.

To remarry or not remarry is a personal choice. It is often contingent upon the available candidates. Over the age of 50, the field is more sparsely populated. We will talk more about this area in another chapter.

"I'll never remarry" is a myth, usually self-induced. It can be popped by keeping the doors to your heart open and your life growing.

Myth number five: "My children will fall victim to my divorce."

This generally means that a divorce will have negative connotations over the years in the life of one's children. Either they will become delinquents and follow a negative lifestyle or they will never marry because of the disillusionment they have witnessed in their parent's marriage.

It is true that children of all ages are affected by divorce. But it can either be a positive effect or a negative one. Over the years I have worked with a number of parents who have carefully guided their children through divorce country and brought them out successfully on the other side. Perhaps we believe too many of the statistics we read in the papers. Children are people long before they become statistics.

Good parenting must go on for years postdivorce. It is a great deal of hard work that seems endless. It surely does not end with divorce papers. It really starts there.

It is a myth to believe that your children will fall victim to your divorce. But the myth can become a reality if you quit parenting somewhere along the divorce-country trail.

Myth number six: "I'll starve to death."

Few people die of physical malnutrition in the years after a divorce, but some do shrivel up due to mental and emotional malnutrition. A man living beyond divorce chooses to live on frozen dinners, eat out, starve, or learn to cook. I am amazed at how many have chosen the latter. Self-responsibility says, "I will do what I need to do to live." This doesn't mean that you simply go in pursuit of someone to do your cooking for you. It means that you learn the process and grow because of it. I don't believe that the only reason women were put here on earth was to cook for and feed men!

This myth usually doesn't affect women, but it does appear to hover over many men in the years after a divorce. Recognize it as a myth and get on with the cooking class. You may be in the kitchen for a while.

Myth number seven: "My house and car will disintegrate."

Many women have pursued the art of housekeeping and housecleaning, but few have specialized in house maintenance. A realtor friend told me that she always knew the houses on a street where a divorce was taking place by the condition of the yard. A mechanic friend said the same thing about automobiles and divorce. They may or may not be correct, but many women have expressed a hopelessness in taking care of house and auto after a divorce. If it was always done by the man of the house, then you will simply have to learn. Classes are offered at colleges in both these categories. Those who have learned have a strong feeling of pride in their accomplishment. Again, it is a myth that can be a reality if not dealt with constructively and creatively.

Myth number eight: "Everyone is always looking at me."

A lady told me of her experience in going to Sunday worship after her divorce experience. She commented that she always looked for a seat in the back of the auditorium because she felt everyone was staring right through her when she took a seat near the front. Thinking that everyone is thinking about you is a mild form of paranoia. It is not uncommon to assume that you are the topic of discussion among other people when you go through a difficult time that has become common knowledge. Divorce news travels faster than poison ivy. It doesn't end with the final papers. It filters through the postdivorce years wrapped up in the sentence, "Did you know that he's (she's) divorced?" Some days you wonder if you will ever be known by any other description.

Divorce, even after many years, bears a stigma. When the word is even spoken, mental images punctuated by human question marks pop into minds. The "I wonder what really happened there?" question can never be answered to everyone's satisfaction. Nor should it be. Perhaps it's not so much that they are looking "at you." It's more what they're wondering *about* you.

It is easy to be self-occupied with the "everyone" thought. The painful part of this is that if you believe it, you will go into hiding. In truth, everyone is not looking at you or thinking about you. Some people will, but you cannot stop that. Let people's looks and thoughts be their own. They need not paralyze you. Get rid of the myth if it's part of your baggage. It will only keep you trying to answer the questions of other people when you cannot hear them being asked. And you will never be able to answer them to everyone's satisfaction even if they were verbalized.

Myth number nine: "I feel like a second-class Christian."

I have lost track of the number of times people have shared this feeling with me. In the words of one man, "Bank robbers and murderers are in better shape in our church than divorced people. The first two can be forgiven, the last one cannot." Our attitude toward the sin of another person can drop him from first- to second-class in the blink of an eye.

Most divorcing people know that divorce is wrong and that it was not a part of God's perfect plan of one husband / one wife, for life. Most divorcing people agree that God had a great plan. For them, for many reasons, it did not work out. Should they now be reduced to living a second-class existence in church and Christian community? I don't believe so. If I did, I would not be working in the divorce recovery area, and *Growing Through Divorce* would not have been read by over a million people in the past eight years.

Many divorced people live with the guilt of their divorce for years to come. Although they have experienced God's forgiveness, the release of guilt feelings takes time. Feelings of guilt lead to feelings of loss of self-esteem. Loss of self-esteem tells a person that he is "not good enough." Other people are always better than he is.

How does a divorced person feel when told after seven years of divorce that he cannot serve on a church board as an elder? How does a divorced woman feel when told she cannot teach a Sunday school class? It makes one wonder if this is a contagious disease or if God's forgiveness is anywhere in the ball park with man's forgiveness. There are scores of committed Christians sitting on the sidelines of Christian community because someone has treated them as a second-class Christian due to their divorce.

Fortunately, churches and religious denominations across America are beginning to realize that their job in the divorce area is not judgment and penalty but mercy and the reconstruction of lives. The feeling of "second class" will be around for a long time to come. My caution is not to fall victim to it. If God worked on the scale of first- and second-class, He would have given Jesus a little better lineage than being born of David's family tree. Some other Old and New Testament characters would also have been in deep trouble.

Confession and forgiveness make for a new person. When God makes you new, you cannot be second-class! If you bought this myth and picked up its feeling, get rid of it right now!

Myth number ten: "It's too late to start over."

You were married for 27 years. You have been divorced for the past eight. Have you started over?

You can insert your own numbers into those two statements. The big question is whether you are really living or just existing. I mentioned in another chapter about the person who told me she was "stuck." Stuck people just get mired and bogged down wherever they are. They don't look to the years beyond divorce as a whole new starting-over experience. They feel they are too old, too tired, too out of gas, too set in their ways, too many years married to now embrace singleness.

It is a good thing for you and me that Colonel Sanders didn't think he was too old to start something new. Kentucky Fried Chicken got going when he was in his sixties! Apparently nobody told him he was over the hill.

This last myth comes from two sources—those voices around us and that small squeaky voice within us. The outside voices have arbitrarily decided that we should stay as we are or simply quit. And many people succumb to those voices. There is no better way to quit than to hang around with those who have quit.

Some older singles' audiences that I address seem to have a zombielike quality to them. They act as though embalmed with a numbness that prohibits growth. They almost become incensed if someone dares move their life ahead. For them, divorce appears to be spelled *death*. Many of them have been divorced for nine, ten, or eleven years.

The inside voice comes from what we tell ourselves. It says, "I can't do that." It may be based on past failures or fear of future failures.

Remember Moses? God called him back into service when he was *80 years old*. He told God he had already been to Egypt and certainly did not want to return. He tried to talk God into sending his brother Aaron because he could communicate better. Moses, unknown to himself, was about to embark upon the most exciting 40 years he had ever known. He used the "not-me" argument with God but it just didn't work, and he finally went equipped with God's promises. You know how the story came out.

Starting over doesn't mean remarriage, although that

might happen. It doesn't mean having babies again, although that has happened to a few. It does mean that you refuse to live in limbo and become a statistical single. It means that all your options are open and that you have chosen to really live beyond divorce.

Not starting over is a myth. It is a myth that can turn you into an observer rather than a participant in new beginnings. Ask God for help to no longer march in place but to get started down the road.

To Think About...

1. Of the ten myths listed in this chapter, which one do you identify most closely with and why?

2. Where have you found "understanding" in your growth beyond divorce?

3. Has any one of these myths become more of a reality to you? Why and how?

4. Do you feel like a first-class Christian or a second-class

Christian right now? Describe why you feel the way you do.

5. How have you "started over" in your life?

Chapter 6

Parenting
Beyond Divorce

Do you remember when your biggest parenting hurdle involved getting your firstborn child to finally sleep through the night? You felt like peace and tranquillity had taken up permanent lodging in your home or apartment once that happened. But the next hurdle soon appeared. When will we get junior out of diapers and into civilized clothes? It seemed to take forever. Finally triumph, only to be followed or preceded by learning to walk, and later, going to school. New hurdles kept appearing as the journey progressed: graduating from grade school, graduating from junior high, getting a driver's license, graduating from senior high, moving out, moving back in, moving out again, finding a career, changing careers—even getting married and getting unmarried.

We could add another 50 hurdles to the child-raising process and quickly realize that the process is unending. It does not matter if you are a divorced parent or a still-married parent—the race through child-raising has the same twists and turns for all of us.

The role and the responsibility of parenting does intensify beyond the divorce experience. Many parents don't realize that you don't divorce your children. When divorces are finalized and processed, you still have the threads of parenting in your hands. That process continues in varied form for the remainder of your life.

In the first two or three years after a divorce, there often seems to be too much parenting or too little. Finding the balance and the key to parental relationships with children postdivorce is never easy. It means making mistakes and offering apologies. It means struggling for words to express accurate feelings. It means striking a balance between the too-much and the too-little parenting. It also means allowing time for your children to readjust to you and what you will be to them in the single-parent role.

I am often asked the question, "Who has it the toughest, the mother or the father?" The answer has two prongs. The first is *both* of them. The second is that it depends on the personal responses of each parent in each situation. The single-parent role postdivorce demands numerous adjustments by both parents. If the adjustments are made, great single parenting is the result. If they are ignored, one parent or the other will usually carry most of the load.

Several things cause a parental role to weaken in the years after a divorce. The first involves loss of continual contact with a child. The more empty space that accumulates between parent and child, the easier it is to ignore the responsibility. The second factor involves the pursuing of other interests by the parent. This can range anywhere from hobbies, careers, or romantic involvements to the selfish pursuit of personal pleasures. A third reason involves a parent getting involved with another person's family. You don't have to be remarried for this to happen; it often happens during the dating process. The urge to impress people and win their affections can involve spending time with their children. This can be a robber of key time with your own family. If marriage in this situation becomes a reality, the quality time for one's own children can rapidly diminish. A fourth cause for a weakening relationship is financial. Receiving or collecting child support payments has gained national recognition in the past few years. New state laws are being enacted to collect unpaid payments.

The financial is always a tough area to deal with. Child support must be viewed not as a penalty to be paid as a result of a divorce but a privilege to be shared to take care of the children that you helped create. I must confess to a short fuse with fathers who neglect child support payments. In most cases it is the child who really suffers. I know there are some extenuating circumstances, but in many cases it is simply not caring or not loving enough to care.

Too many children have gotten the message over the years from a parent that they simply are not important. Making them feel loved and important is a long-term postdivorce responsibility. It is not easily dismissed.

There is a fifth cause for a parent-child relational decline. It is geographical and happens when the noncustodial parent moves a great distance from the child and allows the miles to build a barrier. This is not to say that moves are all bad. Some have to happen for numerous reasons, but each must be weighed carefully in the light of ongoing parenting.

A final cause can often come not from the parent but from the child. If a child, for whatever reasons, rejects the parent postdivorce, the parent will sometimes stop trying and allow the relationship to die. I have seen this happen in numerous instances. It is hard initially to clear out the cobwebs of misunderstanding after a divorce. It takes time to regroup and rebuild what is often torn down in a divorce. Anger, hurt, and rejection are felt by both parent and child. My advice is to take time to build the new bridges and go for the long haul. You can't force relationships, but you can renew them.

A continuing relationship postdivorce is the responsibility of both parent and child. Each must have the freedom to pursue it.

Healthy Relationships with Children

There are nine key areas in building healthy and growing relationships with children in the postdivorce years. They are goals to work on. They are the composite ideas that have come from many single parents that I have talked with across this country.

1. *Weigh carefully where you will live in the postdivorce years.*

This is important whether you are the custodial or the noncustodial parent. Sometimes the noncustodial parent feels that he or she has the freedom to move across the world. You may feel the freedom, but how will that freedom affect your child in the long run?

Both parents should be able to talk about this kind of decision. I know it is not always easy, and I am raising the ideal here. Since I am a strong advocate of the child needing both parents in his or her life, a joint decision might be better than a solitary one. There are strong advantages in both living close and living away from a child. Living away can deliver one from being an entertainer parent and a constant combatant in the postdivorce wars that often set a record for longevity. Fifty-two Saturdays a year might better fit two summer months of concentrated time with a parent living out-of-state. The struggle with this is that a distant parent misses out on the "dailies" in a child's life; homework, ball games, birthdays, the flu, boyfriends, and girlfriends, to name just a few.

After many years of working with divorced people, I am not sure that there is a win or lose position in this. Every situation must be evaluated on its own, and the good of every child must be considered. Sometimes quality of time is better than quantity. I have seen people live out the far and the close with equal success. Sometimes both have to be tried to find out which is best.

The teenage years are strong years of memory-making. They are also times of important decision-making and direction-planning. During these years a child may want to live with a parent whom they have not been around much in past years. In a sense they are reclaiming a parent lost to them. I have witnessed some heartwarming reunions after many years of touch-and-go contact.

Things change and people change in the years after a divorce. A growing person allows that freedom—in fact, welcomes it.

2. *Make ongoing financial support a priority for your children in the postdivorce years.*

I stated earlier that this should be a privilege, not a penalty. Resentment to support is justified if the children do not receive it and the custodial parent squanders it. There is usually a way through the legal process to make sure that the children receive the support. I think the strongest statement here is in saying to a child or children, "I care about you and am willing to see that your needs are met." This is not only the day-to-day new sneakers and Levi's provision. It deals with plans for education and career-training. It says to a child, "I will continue to love you right down the road of life."

Most of the nonsingle parents I know seem to understand that helping a child financially may not even end when they marry. Support goes with the territory. Divorce does not mean financial severance. It means that two adults have chosen (sometimes only one) to not live together in marriage any longer. You don't divorce your children!

I recently read that two-thirds of all single parents who have custody of their children do not receive any child support. I wonder what kind of message is being sent to those children.

3. *Remember special events in the life of your children.*

A celebration for only one person is not very exciting. Birthdays, graduations, sports finals, awards ceremonies, and Christmas are but a few of the special things in a child's life. Most children want their parents to be proud of them. The best expression of that is to be a part of the celebration. I am amazed at the number of parents who forget the special things. Time and distance can very quickly blot out the things you underline in your memory. Remembering is saying "I love you" at special times. It is making little things into big things. It is emphasizing the importance of personhood and the dates that mark its progress.

One of the really hard times in the after-divorce life is the special time of the marriage of a son or daughter. It usually means a visual, psychological, emotional, and mental confrontation with a former spouse as you involve yourself in wedding plans and wedding celebration. Special times like these often cause your memory file to dump its contents all over you. Thoughts of the things that might have been can be overwhelming at this special time. Getting through it all can be the toughest assignment you have had in many a year.

A close second to a wedding is the birth of a grandchild. It brings back the memories of the birth of your own child and the marriage that made it possible. It can literally be history on parade in your life. It is a joyous time but a difficult time as well.

Sometimes the question is, "Do I go or do I stay?" "Do I get involved or do I sit back?" I have learned that there are important times when you are simply needed by your child and you have to respond to their needs rather than your own. Parenting at best is servant work. Serving is putting the needs of others before your own. Serving is being there when it's not easy!

4. *Remember the importance of touch!*

There are three ways that we touch the lives of other people. Physical touch is the first and primary way. We learn of its importance and comfort in infancy. If you grow up in a home where touching is a way of life, it comes easy and seems very natural. If the opposite is true, touch can be a fearful and unnatural thing. Even the phone company tells us to "reach out and touch someone." Sometimes that someone is our own child. A divorce can build high walls that makes touching extremely difficult. A loving touch or a hug can help remove those walls. Older children of divorce may need that touch even more than younger ones. Age does not remove the need. It often intensifies it.

The second way is vocal. Without vocal communication life would come to a standstill. Yet at critical times when communication is desperately needed, many of us go begging for the right words, any words that we can speak. I know many fathers who live miles apart from their children after divorce but never miss a week without several telephone calls being exchanged. They have learned the importance of talking with their children about anything, everything, and nothing. Effective communication with children both young and old is an art. A parent's voice coming over the miles to a child is a message of care and love. It assures them that they are important.

The parent living up close to his or her child after divorce may find it necessary to make time in the daily grind of life to grab some talk time over a hot fudge sundae. Life has a way of unraveling if you don't stay caught up with it. Verbal communication helps us do that. Staying in touch over the years of a divorce takes real effort, but children of all ages need it desperately. How long has it been since you talked with yours?

The third ingredient of touch is getting in touch with feelings. We can hug, talk, talk, and hug, but if we are not in tune with the feelings of our children, we will miss who they really are and how they connect to life. I am amazed at how many parents never talk through their divorce with their children. They feel that it is not the child's business even though it drastically affects his or her life. Many schools are offering afterschool meetings with staff counselors so that children going through divorce will have a forum to express their feelings. That's good and helpful, but it also needs to happen with the parents. It still needs to be done years after a divorce. Feelings can be buried for years. The process of expression helps identify those feelings. Fear is released when feelings are shared. Perhaps parents fear a child's judgment on their action, so they dodge the "How do you feel about this?" question.

I have urged some parents after ten years of divorce to go back and have a feeling exchange with their children even if they are living in their own marriage now. Those who have done it have felt a release and renewal with their children.

Another way of sharing feelings is in the form of a letter. Some people write better than they verbalize. Living at a distance or living up close to a child after divorce, written communication can still build bridges relationally. Everyone likes to receive mail, whether hand-delivered, postage-delivered, or tucked under a pillow.

5. *Surround yourself with memories!*

When I am in someone's home or office, I always look around and see if his or her family is in evidence. Photographs, awards certificates, drawings are all evidences of a relationship. They are a connecting link to the people in our lives that count.

This is especially important for the single parent living miles from his or her children. Updated pictures in baseball uniforms and cheerleading outfits keep the child on center stage in our life. Things made in shop or classroom become the memorabilia of our soul. It is easy to be detracted by all the other symbols in life. Out of sight, out of mind can too easily sever us from our responsibilities.

The other side of the memories if you are a single parent is to give your children the things that will keep you on center stage in their lives. And I don't mean a new car, although it might do the trick for a few. Your photo, your collectibles, your favorite things will help let your child know that you are there with him in a tangible way.

6. *Give the gift of time*

I will long remember the young girl who came into my office in tears many years ago. She waved a hundred-dollar bill in my face and said her father tossed it at her on his way out the door that morning and said, "Have a happy birthday. I'm real busy." As she crumpled it up in her hand, she looked up at me and said, "I just wanted some of his time!"

How many children of all ages have been robbed of time with their parents! All parents, whether single or still married, need to know the importance of spending time with their children. I believe that some of the best quality time is spent on a one-to-one situation, away from other children or family members. The gift of time says, "You are important and special." I wonder as I write this how many children would trade a whole summer vacation from school for a few days with a parent. That's a gift you can't buy.

During this same summer many children will be passed from one single parent to another because the court ruled that way. Some parents will send them the message that they are simply complying with the court order and that they will be happy when it's all over. How do you think a child feels in this situation? Unwanted and unloved, a victim of a divorce they did not want.

There is a big difference in fulfilling the laws of the land and meeting the requirements of love. Living and parenting beyond divorce is a lot more than playing musical children!

7. *Remember that children are a priority.*

The voices of priorities scream loudly at us each day. We have a difficult time answering their call. In the land beyond divorce, priorities tend to lean toward the personal or the "me." Sometimes it's the difference between surviving or drowning. It is hard to think of yourself and your children at the same time. Many single parents have a hard time finding the balance point. Some just forget the kids and worry about themselves. Others forget their own needs and live for their children. Balance is saying out loud, "My children are a priority to me whether they live with me 24 hours a day or not."

The courts in many states have struggled to convince divorcing parents that shared or joint custody is in the best interest of the children. They are trying to make the children a priority of both parents in the world beyond divorce. The sooner parents accept this and work toward it, the better children will live through and after divorce. There are many ways to let a child know that he or she is a priority. Some we have already mentioned in this chapter. Others will come to you as you think about this priority.

8. *Be aware of role changes.*

Living as a single parent beyond divorce means that you will go through some role changes as you adjust to your children's growth. The initial change of going from a parent team to a parent singular is dramatic enough. It takes a few years to readjust your parenting concepts after divorce. It is difficult to know when both parenting heads should make a decision for a child or when one parent can make the decision and run with it. For many parents this is muddy water that never quite clears up.

A parent's role changes a little more when the other spouse chooses to remarry. All of a sudden there are *three* parents making decisions. Add another marriage and there are now *four* parents deciding what one child should or should not do. It gets rather complicated.

Still another role change takes place when a child marries and in-laws come aboard the listing parental ship. You just add two more to the process and now you have *six*! Six parents for one child can really be overload. It happens to many people in the land beyond divorce. It will take major adjustments and vast quantities of patience, but it doesn't put everyday living beyond your reach.

9. *Remember that your children are the rearview mirror to your former spouse.*

In the years after a divorce, many former spouses fade from view. They move on with their lives as you move on with yours. Memories are filed, hurts are healed, new growth and new life begin. Yesterday only reappears when you one day remind your daughter that she acts just like her mother once did. Usually this is not a compliment, and it hurts both the speaker and the hearer.

All children carry the inherited traits of both parents in their being. The *good* is what they want to know and what we want to confirm. The bad both want to forget. It is hard not to pick up the negative reflections of a former spouse in a child. It is safest to recognize them silently rather than audibly. They come up in many ways at many different times. Be careful how you compare and transplant images!

Parenting at a distance and parenting up close go on in the years after a divorce. They can be handled poorly or properly. Proper handling takes a general cooperation on the side of both parents. Divorce battles cannot and should not be fought for years through the children. You can do one thing to end it if you are in that kind of battle: Simply quit the battle. Announce that your part in it is over. At times you have to let your children know this as well. Older children can be used by one parent or the other to keep stirring up the seeds of conflict. Remember, it usually takes two to keep fanning the flame.

Your children deserve a healthy and growing relationship with you in the years after a divorce. You deserve a healthy and growing relationship with them. Make this your goal, and both of you will enjoy the results!

To Think About...

1. Share with your group some of the joys and heartbreaks you have experienced in parenting beyond divorce.

2. Would you remarry someone whom your children, whether young or old, did not approve of? Why or why not?

3. What has helped your relationship with your children grow in your postdivorce years?

4. What do you wish you would have done differently with your children since your divorce?

5. How do you express love to your children?

Chapter 7

The Relational
Roller Coaster

A single-again friend recently told me that his early days of moving back into the singles' world reminded him of being turned loose in a candy store as a kid. His view was summed up in the words of the bumper sticker, "So many women, so little time." He related that he dated furiously and frantically with no specific objective in mind. He desperately wanted acceptance after his own wife rejected him.

Put 200 singles in a room with the same objective and it is little wonder that the media calls singles' gatherings "meat markets," "swap meets," "body factories," etc. The need to realign one's self-esteem and self-worth through the acceptance and affirmation of other people is understandable. The struggle is to find the right way to do it by releasing the panic and working on the possibilities.

The need for relationships started back in the Garden of Eden, first between God and Adam and then between Adam and Eve. Adam's need was simply defined as companionship. In Genesis 2:18 we read, "And the Lord God said, 'It is not good that man should be alone; I will make him a helper comparable to him.' "

We could update that verse into today and say, "It is not good that single persons should be alone." This doesn't mean that all single-again persons need a husband or a wife. Some do and some do not. It *does* mean that all singles need to have meaningful relationships with members of the same sex and of the opposite sex. In order to have those kinds of relationships, a person has to learn to be a risk-taker. The danger of relational risking is getting another dose of rejection rather than a new friend. Not everyone wants to be our friend, nor do we want to be everyone else's friend.

Singles' groups are often looked upon as good places to build new relationships. The larger the group, the greater the potential for bringing new friends into your life. Singles' groups can also become relational disposals. You can use and abuse relationships with the opposite and the same sex until you become emotionally and relationally wasted. Some singles' groups are littered with men and women who have been used and discarded by others. When this happens, the protective shield of self-preservation falls over you and you start keeping people at arm's-length. The choice is to isolate and insulate rather than relate. Can I share with you some discoveries I have made in working with single-again people in building healthy relationships?

First, look at the meeting of every new person as the possible acquisition of a new friend. Too many people scan the surface of a person at first meeting, run through their list of likes and don't likes, and move on to someone else. Some people are only in the business of using others, and if they feel they cannot do that, they move on. Still others ask the question, "What can this person do for me?" rather than the question, "What can I do for this person?" Too few of us think about serving others. Our most frequent desire is to be served.

It takes time to build a friendship; you seldom do it in a first encounter. Sometimes we feel the vibes are right and we feel an emotional click. At other times we feel nothing and too quickly move on.

The relational agenda for a person down the road in divorce country seems to go like this upon first meeting: "Are you a potential date and an eventual life partner?" It is not asked out loud. It is played in stereo in your mind. Often if the answer is no, any possible friendship-building is out of the question. Perhaps a better question is, "Is this person a potential friend and an eventual close friend?" This kind of thought opens the right door and makes you a friend-hunter rather than a headhunter.

Every person in life can stand to expand his or her friendship circle. Few rooms in a person's life are over-crowded with the right kinds of people. The years beyond divorce are years for rebuilding community. Don't always look at them through the temporary lens of transition.

Second, build friendships with members of both sexes. I have listened to too many women tell me they need men in their lives as friends first and foremost, but men seem to have a fear that friendship is only a short step from another marriage. It's true that some women (and some men) do have marriage on the top of their daily agenda. But many simply do not. Assuming things that are not so is often the prelude to fear. Don't assume that everyone wants to get married. If you are in doubt, ask. Don't be afraid to also state that marriage is not on your agenda, but good friendship is. Sometimes the relational air has to be cleared before a solid friendship can begin.

I have discovered that men want to have women in their

lives who will simply be friends to them and nothing more. Women want the same thing. Somehow we need to enable people to do this and talk more freely about it to one another.

I realize that many marriages come from basic friendships. There are few guarantees that they will or will not happen. The safeguard is that you have a choice and need not marry someone if you choose not to.

Some men and women are afraid to build opposite-sex relationships due to the hurts they experienced from a husband or wife in their divorce. I have listened to the line "All men are . . . all women are . . ." too many times. It is an indictment that usually stems from the wounds collected in a first marriage. Don't allow anyone to put you in a box!

One long-divorced person recently summed up for me her success in relationship-building by stating that she probably could not afford to remarry. She had acquired so many men as warm personal friends that a new spouse would probably not allow her to keep those friendships. Then she told me that it took about seven years for her to fill her life with that kind of friendship circle. She had worked at rebuilding her supportive community and was now enjoying it.

Third, avoid using a relationship to simply fill the holes in your own life. Some people have a hard time discovering that things are to use and people are to enjoy. Too many have that in reverse order. Pain causes us to use people. The right person, and sometimes even the wrong person, can get our mind off the pain.

Panic causes us to use people. The fear of being alone temporarily or forever can push you to use people to fill the void. Hurt also can cause you to use people to fill the hole. When a person is hurting, he is most emotionally vulnerable to another person. The other person can quickly become the Band-Aid for the hurt. Rejection in a marriage can push a person to become a people-collector. A long parade of people drifting in and out of your life simply fills the holes and plugs the gaps temporarily.

Filling the holes left by another person is never an easy chore. No one would want to be known as a "hole-filler." The key in a healthy relationship is to know that you are special in a special way to a special person.

Fourth, realize that most of the relationships we make in life are of the temporary variety. Few people will ever attain the "intimate" relationship category with most of us. Intimacy demands time, sharing, caring, and commitment. You can never achieve that with a crowd. In my book *Suddenly Single* I speak about the three circles of relationships as being random, social, and deep. Another definition would be casual, close, and intimate. We have all three groups ambling through our lives. Even deep relationships can be deep for a short time and then move out of our life. We have to learn to receive what we can from them while we have them, and then allow them to pass on to someone else.

Remember when you were a child or a teenager and had a best friend for a few years? Finally that friend moved away to a distant state. You vowed you would be friends forever and sealed it in blood. You wrote back and forth every day for weeks, called on weekends, and kept the memory alive. But slowly the relationship faded, and after a year or less it was all but dead. Question? How should you feel when that happens to you, both back then and right now? Sad, disappointed, rejected, lied to? I believe the right word is *fortunate*—glad you had the friendship when you did, so that you will never forget what it was to you when you had it. I call that receiving life from a vital friendship and allowing it to pass along to someone else down the road. It wasn't time wasted. It was time captured and transferred into helping you grow in life. Seldom is a great friendship a waste of time. It is an investment of time.

Life in the postdivorce journey can easily become a

series of fleeting relationships. I hope you won't be traveling so fast that you miss the relationships that can make a vital contribution to your life. Allow them to be God's messenger to you and perhaps His angel unaware while they are in your life. Allow them to pass along when it is time for you and for them to move on. You can never strangle a healthy relationship. You have to give it freedom to breathe!

Fifth, watch out for relational messiahs. They are the people handing out cards with the words "Have I got a deal for you!" on them. They are often the "rescuers" who, once they have a hand on you, manage to pull you down rather than lift you up. They have their own agenda and are really not too interested in yours. Many of them are loaded with charm, good looks, fashionable clothes, fine automobiles, and mysterious vocations. They swoop in and out of lives like an early morning fog. They come garbed as *men and women*. I want to make sure you understand that. Too many women think that only men are bent on this preoccupation. Numerous women are also out there looking for wounded men to take under their wing.

A relational messiah is probably the most dangerous person in any singles' group or singles' organization. Christian singles' groups have an abundance of them. The only difference from the ones in the secular setting is that the Christian variety use a lot of religious words and hang around church parking lots.

It is easy to build a friendship with a relational messiah. All you have to do is shake hands or exchange a nod. He or she will do the rest.

Even some "good guys" have a tendency to fall into this category. In their own desire to be accepted, they specialize in spreading their wings over others.

The cautious word here is simply *watch out!* If you are awake and aware, you will recognize them at a distance.

Sixth, don't make the mistake of believing that a sexual relationship outside of the context of marriage has a moneyback or money-in-the-bank guarantee.

One of the most frequent questions asked by single-again persons is, "How do I deal with sexuality and singleness?" I always cringe when I hear the question coming because I realize only too well the struggle that causes it to be asked. Lately I have wondered if the real question isn't phrased this way: "Is having a sexual relationship outside of marriage a guarantee that you might marry the person you have the relationship with?"

I meet a great many singles who confess to being used sexually because they had the idea that the relationship was moving toward marriage. They felt they would be drawn together humanly if they experienced a sexual relationship. Only later did they find out that this was not true.

There are many different attitudes in our society in dealing with the sexual question. In *Suddenly Single* I present the basic three attitudes that most people identify with. The third is summed up in this way: I believe that sex and sexuality are a gift of God and are best enjoyed within the context of a marital relationship. It is my belief that if more single-again people ascribed to that view, there would be a lot less confusion in this area. They would have an attitude based on a biblical reality, one that would not be placed on the block in exchange for a marriage guarantee.

Some singles use a sexual encounter to hang onto a relationship. Others simply use it to gratify their own needs. It is no guarantee of intimacy, endurance, or longevity. Healthy relationships demand more than rumpled sheets. Single people are no different from married people. We all need to be surrounded by healthy relationships so we can become the people God meant for us to be.

Seventh, take the time to shape up your life to the point where you are presenting a relationally attractive *you*. This usually means going to work on your *person*. Most of us take a lot of time to look good to others from the outside. Packaging works well in the eye-appeal market of the world. On the human side, we need to make sure that there is something there when our wrapping is taken off.

Learning to communicate is one key to developing the inner person. Much of the talk during marriage is maintenance talk. Not much of it is soul-talk or feeling-talk. Learning to express feelings in conversation is one way we let people know who we are on the inside.

Learning to listen is another key to relating to other people. Do you specialize in monologues or dialogues when you are with friends? We listen in two ways: with the ears of our head or the ears of our heart. Most people can tell which set we are using.

Learning to be a person for others helps draw people around you. Self-centered people usually push people away. Being there for others at strategic times and having others there for you when you need them is vital to growing relationships.

We could continue the list for several more pages, but I think you get the idea. We are talking about inside stuff. Take a look at yourself and ask what kind of *you* is being seen by other people.

Eighth, look at a new friendship as an opportunity for the giving and receiving of gifts. Giving-and-receiving is the two-way street in relationship-building. Sharing our gifts in that context is simply passing on what God has passed out to us. Some of those gifts are trust, affirmation, availability, confidence, love, accountability, and encouragement. These are but a few; there are really hundreds. We may not think of them as gifts because they appear intangible. They are not easily defined, and they cannot be wrapped and presented. They are woven into the fabric of living and appear in the light of real friendship.

Too often a friendship is viewed from the receiving rather than the giving perspective. Many gifts go unwrapped in a friendship because we question the value to the recipient. It is only when we offer them freely that other people can be the beneficiary. The greater the time invested in building a friendship, the greater the quality and value of the gift shared.

Ninth, learn to become an "interesting" person to others. I am always fascinated when I discover boring people who think they are interesting and interesting people who think they are boring. Being an interesting person demands a degree of openness and vulnerability. It involves being a risker in new areas of life and living. It is doing something you have not done before and inviting someone to take the journey with you. It is asking questions and listening for the answers. It is reading newspapers, magazines, books, and people.

Of all your friends, how many would you classify as interesting? What makes them interesting and why do you enjoy their company? Are you one of *their* interesting friends?

Tenth, spend time building brother-sister relationships. We have talked about man-woman relationships on a friendship-only level. We have talked about dating-mating relationships. Both are a part of living as a single person in the years beyond divorce. I believe there is a third kind of relationship that can develop if you will work on it. It is similar to the man-woman friendship but has a spiritual quality and depth to it that makes it very special.

The Bible teaches that we become a member of God's family by receiving Christ into our life as our Lord and Savior. It's called the new birth. When that happens to us, we not only become a member of the family of God, but we become brothers and sisters to all who joined a little before we did. In *Growing Through Divorce* we speak of three kinds of families in life. There is the one you were born into, your natural family. There is the one you married into. And then there is God's family, the one we have just spoken about. The first two can change in an instant. The last is permanent.

The biggest family in the world is God's family. *All* the members are your brothers and sisters. A whole new light on relationships dawns when we begin to look around and really see who our brothers and sisters are. The way we treat them changes. The way we talk with them changes. The way we view them changes. The way we value them changes. They are not a sea of passing faces; they are our brothers and sisters, and we are a brother or sister to them.

The next time you are with a group of your friends, remind yourself that this is your family. A lot of things will change in how you relate to them.

Life and the building of solid relationships can often have a roller-coaster effect. There are the highs and the lows, the twists and the turns, the scary parts and the calm parts. Most of all, there is the excitement of the ride. Least of all, you don't want to take the ride alone.

One more thing. Remember what Pogo said in the comic strip: "We have met the enemy, and they is us!" Sometimes we are our own worst enemy in building relationships. We push people away rather than draw them to us. If you find yourself doing that, get some help and head in a new direction!

To Think About...

1. How do you view potential new relationships in your life—use and discard or collect and save?

2. How many close friends do you have of the opposite sex? How can you build that kind of friendship?

3. What are your secrets of building friendships?

4. Do you have all the friends you can handle?

5. Why do you feel a person would want you as a friend?

Chapter 8

Learning to Wait

I hate lines! I hate to stand in a line and wait for it to disappear in front of me. I feel that waiting in line is a giant waste of my time, and I don't know what to do while I'm standing there waiting. I find myself going to great lengths to avoid lines. When the traffic is moving too slowly on our California freeways, I try to dodge around the congestion on surface streets. Even if it takes longer, I will do it to avoid waiting in line. I leave ball games early so I won't get caught in the congested lines of traffic. I am definitely not a good waiter. But I am a lot better than I used to be.

The Army is often referred to as the place where you "hurry up and wait." Life is a little like the Army: You and I are hurrying here and there but we still find ourselves doing a lot of waiting. Impatience seems to grow with age. We don't want to hurry the end of our journey through life, but we don't want to stand around and wait for the finish line either. Perhaps the secret in a well-balanced life is to know when to hurry and when to wait.

Waiting is never easy. Our basic problem with it is wondering if anything constructive is happening while we are waiting for it to happen. I have heard that there are three kinds of people in life: those who make things happen, those who watch things happen, and those who don't know what's happening. Perhaps we can add a fourth: those who never learn to wait so that the right things can happen.

Solomon, writing in Ecclesiastes the third chapter, tells us that there is a time for everything. He ends his long list with a word of promise in the eleventh verse. It simply says, "He has made everything beautiful in its time."

There is a vast difference between waiting and living in limbo. Limboland is populated by people who cannot use waiting creatively. They simply plop on the curb of life until someone presents them with a game plan. If it fits their lifestyle, they adopt it and move on. If not, they reject it and wait for a better one. They are often pessimists who blame their present state on their past experiences. They carry signs saying, "Wanted! Relational messiah with good credit!"

There seem to be two kinds of single-again people living in the land of divorce—those who are creatively waiting, planning, and moving their lives ahead, and those who are waiting for someone else to do it for them. I want to share some areas where waiting needs to be practiced and perfected in those years.

The first area is waiting for and before the Lord. If you have made a decision in your life to live for God, you will soon learn that you can't live ahead of God. Since He has the plans for your life in His hand, you will have to wait each day until He reveals them. The easiest way to begin this practice is to quietly present yourself to the Lord at the beginning of each new day and simply say, "Here I am, Lord. I'm waiting for Your direction and instructions." And as a friend of mine says, "Then be quiet long enough to hear what God is trying to say back to you." It is easier for most of us to spend our time dictating letters to God rather than receiving His dictation to us.

Isaiah tells us the benefits of waiting before the Lord. In chapter 40 verse 31 he says, "But those who wait on the Lord shall renew their strength; they shall mount up with wings like eagles, they shall run and not be weary, they shall walk and not faint." Most of us forget the waiting; we just take off and start running!

For many people who have been single after divorce for a number of years, it is easy to feel that waiting is all you do. You wait for circumstances to change, you wait for your career to take off or crash, you wait for a special someone to come into your life, you wait for the seasons of life to come and go, you wait to make more money so you can pay more money for things that keep costing more money. You wait for a serendipity that will rescue you from waiting. And you keep waiting while you wait.

I believe you will ease the tensions and burdens of waiting when you center your waiting upon the Lord. When you start there, it puts all the tension and frustration in the Lord's hands. This doesn't mean that you give up; it means that you give in and put waiting in the right perspective. It becomes exciting when you are waiting for the Lord to direct because you know you will get good directions!

I am waiting for the moment when I will finish writing this book. While I am waiting for that, I have to wait daily upon the Lord for His wisdom in writing what He wants written to you. This is not an easy process, but I have found it has worked wonderfully well in my past three books.

Waiting for the Lord to work in your situation will give

you confidence and patience, and will remove fear and panic. As His plan is allowed to unfold in your life, you will realize that "He makes all things beautiful in *His* time." That's not *your* time, that's *His time!*

David the psalmist, talked about his own experiences in waiting before the Lord. In Psalm 40:1-3 he said, "I waited patiently for the Lord, and He inclined to me, and heard my cry. He also brought me up out of a horrible pit, out of the miry clay, and set my feet upon a rock, and established my steps. He has put a new song in my mouth—Praise to our God; many will see it and fear, and will trust in the Lord."

That's a result worth waiting for! God listens for our waiting and then responds with His direction. Getting your feet planted on the rock beats living in the swamp of life. Establishing your steps is far removed from stumbling over your own feet. Singing a new song is a whole lot better than singing your old song off-key.

It all starts with waiting—not just waiting for God to make things happen but for God *to happen* in your life.

The second area of waiting involves waiting for God's healing process to bind up the wounds of your life. I meet many people who have accumulated a varied assortment of wounds in living their lives. You cannot escape hurts if you are living in the real world. Our tendency in dealing with them is to want instant healing. We largely get this attitude from television and media advertisements. We expect a "plop, plop, fizz, fizz, oh what a relief it is!" response to both stomach upset and emotional wounds. When it doesn't happen, we become impatient and discouraged with the healing process and often try to ignore the hurts.

It takes years for all the hurts incurred through a divorce to heal. There are many hurts that follow in the years after a divorce. The things people say and the embarrassment they feel keep many wounds open.

When we learn to wait before the Lord, we also learn

to wait for His healing touch conveyed on His timetable for our life. God does want our hurts to be healed. God's concern for all healing in our lives is revealed in Exodus 15:26: "If you diligently heed the voice of the Lord your God and do what is right in His sight, give ear to His commandments and keep all His statutes, I will put none of the diseases on you which I have brought on the Egyptians. For I am the Lord who heals you." You will notice that this healing results from *listening to the voice of the Lord*. Listening demands waiting. Many hurts go unresolved because we are not willing to collect them, bring them before the Lord, and wait for what He will say to us about them.

Sometimes God walks us through them again in order to effect healing. Sometimes we are simply released from them in a miraculous way. God best understands the process that will aid in our own growth.

Waiting for healing in the emotional and spiritual realm is a patient process. It is far better than trying to run through life with your wounds still dripping! How is your healing process going?

The third area of waiting is waiting for other people. Have you ever prepared a wonderful dinner only to have your guests appear an hour late? Have you ever gotten to a concert late because you had to wait for friends who are never on time? Waiting for others is as difficult for most of us as waiting in line.

We wait for others to become as mature and wise as we are. When that doesn't happen in 60 seconds, we often become impatient and move on to other people. We wait for others to "grow up." We wait for some to "get their act together."

One of the strong things I stress to postdivorce people is to try to build relationships some of the time with other people who are on the same growth level. A second marriage coupling a one-year divorced person to a seven-year divorced person can make for very rough going. The primary reason is the distance between the two in personal growth. I don't suggest that the seven-year person wait for five or six years until the other catches up. The best wisdom might be to look for someone who is closer to where you are.

One of the tougher areas in waiting for others involves children. We want them to grow up, but more than this, we want them to come to a place of understanding where they will know where we are and where we have come from. The struggle is that parents don't want to wait on children and children don't want to wait on parents.

Another area in waiting for others involves understanding and approval. Many divorced people desperately want others to know their struggle and to have people say they love and accept them. Loss of affirmation is often deadly in living beyond divorce. Too many people imply that they really don't care to understand what you have gone through or what you might still be going through. If you are waiting for your church to accept your divorce and love you in spite of it, you may wait for a long time in some cases. We are slowly discovering in the church that divorced people have a right to keep on living after divorce without constant judgment, indictment, and condemnation.

The fourth area of waiting is waiting for myself. We are usually clubbed to death by our impatience in this area. It is one thing to wait on the things outside yourself. It is quite another to wait on the things *inside* yourself. We become easily enslaved with the "Why did I do that?" mentality. From there it is easy to put oneself down and not get up too often.

Most of us are slow growers. We have all seen the sign saying, "Please be patient—God isn't finished with me yet." Perhaps it should say, "I must be patient with me—God isn't finished with me yet."

It is easy to get down on yourself for many reasons. Elijah, after one of his greatest victories in the Bible, ended up crying the blues under a bush.

Waiting for yourself is directly related to waiting on the Lord. If the Lord is working in you, the promise of Philippians 1:6 will become reality: "Being confident of this very thing, that He who has begun a good work in you will complete it until the day of Jesus Christ."

Impatience with yourself is denying the patience of God to be fully explored and absorbed into your life. God teaches us how to wait on the part of us that is so very human and so very real. He does His work slowly and thoroughly. Waiting for yourself is allowing Him that freedom.

Other people will often express their impatience with you as you wait upon the Lord and on yourself. Let that be their problem and not yours. Your greatest danger is pushing the river rather than going with the flow of it. A word directing us in this area comes from Psalm 37:7: "Rest in the Lord and wait patiently for Him." I can wait on myself if I know I am waiting on the Lord.

The fifth area in waiting is waiting for God's timing or God's openings. Too few of us really wait for God to open doors that He wants us to walk through. We are in the habit of opening our own doors and asking God's blessings as we walk through them. Consequently we run into a lot of dead ends and wonder why. The shortest distance between two doorways in life is measured by God's yardstick, not ours.

I have discovered as I grow older that I want to hurry the openings of the doors that remain in my life. Perhaps you have the same problem. It is a good thing that one's age really doesn't mean a whole lot to God. He certainly is never in a hurry and spends a lot of time helping us to change directions and to go where He wants us to go.

The wisdom of Solomon is expressed in Proverbs 3:6: "In all your ways acknowledge Him, and He shall direct your paths." This simply means asking God for directions and allowing him to point out the road or the door. It takes a mature, sensitive Christian, when faced by decision-making pressure, to tell someone that he is waiting for the Lord to open the right door, whether for a job change, a move to a new town or state, a career change, or a relationship change. They are there at different times in all of our lives. How great it is to know that God is leading you in a certain way, and to share this leading with others! How thrilling to know that God has told you to do something but has not told you how He will bring it about!

I believe that God gives us little challenges to trust Him before He gives us big ones. When He knows we are waiting and listening, He is not afraid to speak.

A sixth area of waiting is what many single-again people don't want to wait for but feel they may have to wait forever for: a special someone whom they can marry and enjoy happily ever after. Waiting for that person to appear on the horizon can seem like an endless process. Living in the relational waiting room of life can grind down your endurance and the faith you once had in believing that there is always someone for everyone in life.

I believe there are often some special reasons why that person has not appeared in your life. The first is that God knows that *you* are not ready for the relationship. You may feel ready, think ready, and act ready, but God is saying, "Not yet." Again, waiting for the Lord's timing in this area is tough.

The second reason is that God's special person *for you* isn't ready yet. I know, you would like to know who it is so you can help speed up the process! Let God do it. He knows more about the person than you do.

The third reason is often that your situation or theirs needs to change before either of you will be ready for a relationship. In reality, your preparation process isn't finished yet, nor is theirs.

A fourth reason is that you need more time to grow and build your own life. Most of us are slow learners; and we think we are ready for many things long before their time. The mistake in many second marriages that have crumbled is in the "not ready" and "too soon" categories.

I encourage you to pray for patience and a deeper understanding of God's timing in this area for your life. It certainly is not easy.

Waiting has always been a part of God's plan. Watching the seasons of the year change is a waiting process. Watching your children grow up is a waiting process. Watching the sunrise is a part of waiting for the sunset.

God calls us to become better waiters. I believe we will get things done a whole lot better and perhaps a bit faster if we start out waiting on the Lord. How much waiting have you done lately?

To Think About...

1. Are you a good "waiter"? Why or why not?

2. Share some ways that you have learned how to wait on the Lord.

3. Do you become impatient waiting for those around you to "grow up"? Why?

4. Do you tend to be impatient with yourself? What does that do to you?

5. What doors are you waiting for most eagerly to open in your life?

Chapter 9

Searching for New Things

When was the last time you experienced something totally new in your life? If you are a little like most of the people on our planet, you probably get a little nervous when a friend suggests that you do something you have never done before. Perhaps it's dining at a new restaurant, buying a clothing style that no one would expect you to wear, getting your hair styled in a totally different way, buying the kind of automobile that no one would expect you to drive, or taking skydiving lessons. There is a certain degree of comfort, nostalgia, history, and trust in things we have experienced before. Things yet to be experienced contain a large element of risk, mystery, fear, and nervousness. It is little wonder that many of us revert to past experiences when the option for new things beckons to us.

Sameness can be boring and dull, but it is usually predictable. I have listened to people complain for years about boring worship services, but just try to place the doxology at the end of the service from its traditional place, and see what happens! We fight the battle of wanting change, but not badly enough to risk its uncertainty.

One of the biggest battles that single-again people face in the years after a divorce is making the adjustment from thinking married to thinking single. It is not only a battle of actions but a battle of thoughts and emotions.

It is not easy to slip out of the gear of marriage after 24 years and instantly raise the banner of singleness. I have listened to numerous single people tell me that they still think married after many years of divorce. The letting-go process often depends on the person and the things that person does to move his or her life in a new direction. A friend recently told me that most divorced people need to have a "garage sale of the mind" in the after-divorce years. The mental things stick around long after the material things have been replaced, removed, or reorganized.

One of the strongest calls to living successfully in the years beyond divorce is the call to newness. In over 12 years of working with divorced people, I have discovered that the ones who really grow beyond their divorce are the ones who put newness into their lives in large doses.

I am not suggesting that you sell your furniture, house, car, dog, and clothes, and then resign your job this afternoon to experience newness. That kind of newness is pushed by panic more than by logic and discovery. Those who tend to react rather than act can just add to the logjam in their life. Acting on potential newness in your life usually comes with thoughtful planning. It is promoted by the desire to be challenged by new things, new people, new possibilities. It is a calling forth of the latent pioneer spirit that is hidden away in most of us under the layers of sameness and predictability.

I believe the call to newness comes strongest from the Scriptures. In the Old Testament, God had a way of calling the Israelites to new adventures on a daily basis. He frequently called their leaders to move into areas they had not experienced before. God did not want them to settle down and get rusty!

In the New Testament, the early Christians were caught in a constantly changing fellowship. They were experiencing new life, and that meant releasing the old life forms that they were used to. Even Jesus in His earthly ministry defied predictability. He brought newness wherever He went. He defied tradition and those who embraced it as ultimate truth. The die is cast in the Scriptures: God is in the business of newness.

There are a number of areas of newness in the Scriptures that I believe can challenge you as you review your life and decide to make newness a fellow traveler with you in living beyond divorce.

A New Song

David the psalmist speaks about a new song in Psalm 40:3: "He has put a new song in my mouth—praise to our God." In Psalm 98:1 he says, "Oh, sing to the Lord a new song, for He has done marvelous things!" This Scripture tells us that we have received a new song from God and that we are to sing it. I can just hear you mumbling that you don't have a musical note anywhere in your life and this doesn't apply to you. Music is simply lyrics and harmony blended together to make a song. Songs start with words. Words start with thoughts. Music is communication.

I believe David had two songs in his life. His old song dealt with the problems he had been through, the struggles he had faced, and the defeats he had experienced. You can read all about them in the Scriptures. David's new song is reflected in many of his Psalms. It tells how God gave him victories over defeats and changed his song.

You can spend a lot of time in life singing your old songs and telling your stories of woe, but after a while people get tired of listening. Singing a new song in your life is focusing on what God has done for you, what He is doing for you, and what He will do for you. It is recognizing that He has done marvelous things in your life—that you are no longer the same, and therefore your song is changed. David knew this, and you can know it also.

It is not easy to be a praising person. We are often afraid of being branded a fanatic if we say "Praise the Lord!" when God does something unique and wonderful in our life. When the new song in our life is written by the Master Composer, it will be hard to contain it. The old songs of yesterday will be permanently stored and the new songs of our todays will be happily shared. You don't have to be a singer to share your song. It comes from the open spirit inside you.

New Things

Isaiah was a prophet in the Old Testament. When he wasn't preaching, he was prophesying. When he wasn't prophesying, he was listening to God for instructions. God's word to him one day is found in Isaiah 43:18,19: "Do not remember the former things, nor consider the things of old. Behold I will do a new thing; now it shall spring forth."

I'm sure Israel got tired of hearing about new things. There had been so many of them in their lives that they probably told each other what their forefathers had told Moses: "Let's go back to Egypt—the food was better there." Yet God's adventure for them was in new things, not old ones. The fear of the new and the comfort of the old kept Israel in a state of constant tension, much as it can with you and me.

I believe that God's promise to you and me is that He will do new things that He has not done before in our lives if we will let Him. He doesn't barge into our lives and bang down the walls. He waits for our invitation to allow His new things to be a part of our journey. You are probably thinking, "What new things?" I wish I could give you a list, but I can't. God knows just what we need, and He shares them on His timetable. Because God expects us to use our minds, I believe you have the freedom to make your own list of the new things you would like to see in your life, and then prayerfully ask God's direction in seeing them happen. For you it might be a career or job change. It could mean a geographical change. It could mean some changes on the inside of your life. It could be asking God to bring a special person into your life. The list could be endless. God separates the wants from the needs.

I have been privileged to watch God do new things in thousands of formerly married persons. Sometimes I have been on the playing field of life with them as new things have been introduced. At other times I have merely watched from the sidelines. God is definitely the introducer of new things.

A New Name

When Abram was 99 years old, God decided to give him a new name along with a giant promise. He was to be called "Abraham" and was to become the father of many nations. Simon was doing his best to be a disciple when Jesus changed his name to "Peter" because it meant "rock." Both Abraham and Peter lived up to their new names.

What's in a name? Is it just a handle connected to a person that gives an identity for a driver's license? I have a plaque in my office telling me my name, James, means truthful. That's quite a challenge to live up to!

There is a current trend among many formerly married women to take back their maiden name after divorce. Some have said they don't want to be a second "Mrs." anyone. Others want to reclaim their identity. Perhaps still others want to continue building their life where they left off years earlier when they merged identities in marriage. Some have asked me my opinion of name-reclaiming. In many cases it works well as long as the children don't feel left out in the cold bearing their father's name and having a mother with a different name. I realize that their mother's name could change anyway with a remarriage. This is a highly personal decision that needs to be weighed carefully and prayerfully.

Many people have lost their *identity* in a marriage, not just their name. Reclaiming a name can lead to rebuilding an identity.

We all come into life with a name soon affixed to us. Our challenge is to live out our name in honor and pride. When other names are tied to us, names like *weak, stupid, boring, crazy, failure, out to lunch,* etc., we need to get a name change, to change the brand that other people, and perhaps you yourself, have hung around your neck.

God gave new names to people based on what He saw in them, not on what they were. What does God see in you and what do you see in your name? Is it time for a name change in some area of your life?

A New Spirit

We have just spent two weeks here in Los Angeles being bathed in the spirit of the Olympics. You may have watched some of it on television. It began for us when we lined a street and watched the Olympic Torch go by. We all were saturated with Olympic spirit and American pride in those early-morning hours. It continued as we watched the opening ceremonies. Many of us cried as we became spirit-saturated. It progressed as we stood by a curb and watched the bicycle races and saw the gold medal being presented to an American winner. Through 14 days and nights we watched the spirit of America on parade as many of our Olympians won medals. As it all wound down, I was drained. It was a spiritual experience.

It is hard to define what spirit is. High school cheerleaders have it; long-distance runners have it; moms and dads at Little League games have it. Like an ethereal fog, it drifts around our lives. We are never quite sure what it is, but we certainly know when we don't have it.

The word of the Lord came to the prophet Ezekiel one day: "Then I will give them one heart, and I will put a new spirit within them, and take the stony heart out of their flesh, and give them a heart of flesh" (Ezekiel 11:19). That sounds like what happens when your team is behind by one run with two batters out in the bottom of the ninth inning! Everyone cheers for and supports the batter, hoping he will hit a home run and win the game.

It also sounds like a person who is told he has a debilitating illness that won't get better. At first he may decide to give up, but then he decides to fight. The spirit to give in is replaced with the spirit to get on. A spirit-hardened heart is replaced by a tender one, and a decision is made to fight. It is also a person who has been divorced after 18 years of marriage, and after six years of singleness has not remarried. A "what's-the-use" attitude takes over, and the person falls victim to the past.

But wait. God has stirred up a new spirit within, and you begin to realize that today is the first day of God revealing the rest of His life plan to you. The apostle Paul said it in these words: "We are knocked down, but we are not knocked out."

I have witnessed the world of low spirits in people's lives at the point of divorce. I have watched the "give in" of the spirit. I have seen the "no-hope thermometer" begin to go down. I have also watched the striking of the spark of the spirit in a life and watched that life come alive. A new spirit and a new heart are gifts of God that start you on the road to a new beginning.

A New Commandment

If divorce is anything, it is the decline and fall of love. A relationship born in love often ends in hate. It can cause a person to stay on a hating binge for many years after a divorce. Some people work overtime fanning the fires of hatred toward another person. It takes a great deal of growth to put hatred to rest and witness the rebirth of love in your life.

Jesus was spending some time with His disciples on the Mount of Olives. He was teaching and preparing them for a time when He would no longer be with them. At the center of His teaching He gave His followers a new principle to follow: "A new commandment I give to you, that you love one another; as I have loved you, that you also love one another" (John 13:34). The disciples did not hate one another when Jesus spoke these words. They probably had average relationships going in their small group. Jesus wanted to give them a new basis for their relationships that would draw them even closer in the days ahead. He simply told them to love each other with as much intensity as He loved them. He set the example for love in action.

I believe that this is how we are called as His followers to respond to one another. We may not even be close to that standard in many of our relationships, but love is our goal in all of them. Can I suggest here that one day, down the road, you will again be able to say, "I love my former spouse"? For many people to arrive there, God will have to be directing the process. It doesn't come easily.

Learning to love again, whether it be a former spouse or just an everyday relationship that has soured, is a refining process. For some people that really is a new thing.

Love is the wet cement into which all our footprints should go!

New Mornings

Are you a morning person or an evening person? I think all of civilization falls into one of those two groups. I'm a morning person: the earlier the better. But my battery dies about 9:30 the evening, when the night people are really just getting in gear.

Mornings are looked upon as the dawn of new beginnings. They are an adventure to be invited into. They are starting times—unless you work the night shift.

If life has beginnings and endings, it also has mornings and evenings: ''Through the Lord's mercies we are not consumed, because His compassions fail not. They are new every morning; great is Your faithfulness'' (Lamentations 3:22,23).

The writer simply says that God's love for us is brand-new every morning. How's that for a thought to take into a blue Monday morning with you? God seems to know that we need something from Him to really get our mornings going. Notice that it says *every* morning. No empty mornings with God around!

Sometimes mornings can be translated into days, weeks, and years. There is never a time or place where God cannot be invited to help you start a new morning!

A New Creation

A book when it is finished is a new creation. A stack of blank pages at the beginning is transformed into pages of love and care. A blank canvas to an artist becomes a creation when it is filled with loving brush strokes to make a beautiful landscape. A seven-layer cake is a creation when it comes out of the oven and is ready to be enjoyed.

A life is a creation when it is worked upon day after day and not allowed to rust out due to lack of use and poor care.

We are all artists in creating our lives. Life is never intended to be a series of old endings. In God's creative wisdom, life is always a series of new beginnings.

Each day you and I are new creations. We create and we are created. We affect the creation of those around us as well as our own.

It is easy to look at life as a series of events loosely tied together with leftover string. We all have our list of the Big Ten or Big Twenty events in life. When all the events have taken place, we have a tendency to sit on the curb and watch someone else's events happen. Too many people living in the land beyond divorce are sitting on the curb. They have quit the creating process in their own life and are content to watch others. It's a good way to get moldy!

Paul the apostle wrote a letter to some early Christians. In it he said, "Therefore, if anyone is in Christ, he is a new creation; old things have passed away; behold, all things have become new" (2 Corinthians 5:17). This, for all of us, is the ultimate creation. It happens when we are born into God's family by receiving Christ as our Lord and Savior. When this happens, we are a whole new creation of God. But the creation doesn't stop there. It keeps on going through our entire life. We keep on growing in His love and in the love of those around us.

Have you considered allowing God to make you a new creation? It can happen right this minute as you bow your head and invite Christ into your life. Becoming a new creation is simply giving all you know of yourself to all you know of God. Sometimes that doesn't seem like much but let that be God's problem, not yours.

Something old, something new, something borrowed, something blue. That may work fine for weddings, but in real day-to-day living, my choice would be going for the something new in life. New life in Christ is where it all begins.

To Think About...

1. Do you tend to live in the past, the present, or the future?

2. What new things has God done in your life postdivorce?

3. If you are a woman, how do you feel about taking your maiden name back? If a man, how do you feel about your former spouse taking her maiden name back?

4. What new things have you created in your life in the past year?

Chapter 10

Beyond Divorce
As a Woman

In the past 12 years of working with divorced and widowed men and women, I have tried to be a listener to their struggles and celebrant of their joys. I have gained valuable insight from their shared experiences and have tried to pass them onto other people in the form of hope and helpful knowledge. A few evenings ago I met with eight single women who have been living beyond divorce and death of a mate for an average of eight to thirteen years. We started the evening by asking the question, "What are the struggles and joys for you in the land of being single again?" For the next three hours I listened as they shared. The following is the heart of what was said.

Men!

Where are they and why are they like they are seemed to be the two most unanswered questions of the night. Many of those present seemed to feel that all the good candidates for marriage were already married. Others wondered why men their ages were only interested in dating women 15 years younger than they were. Was it their need for ego reinforcement and their desire to find someone who needed to be taken care of that caused this social imbalance?

The strong need for male companionship was felt by all, not in the sense of beginning a relationship that would eventually lead to marriage but in forming a friendship that would have more of a brother-sister quality to it. It was agreed that this was hard to come by because many men had never experienced this kind of friendship. Some present felt that an impending friendship needed to be defined before it could be misunderstood.

Another concern in this group was that men understand that all women were not looking for the knight in shining armor to rescue them from the lonely-single-lady syndrome. All the women in the group acknowledged having to assume responsibility for themselves after their divorce and in the intervening years, and all felt they had done it well. They were not looking for a rescuer. This may have been true in the first year or two after their divorce, but it was no longer true. Their need levels had changed and their selectivity had climbed up the male scale. The feeling was that men became a little nervous when they were in the presence of a "together" woman. There were no "leftover" pieces that they could assemble.

There was a strong feeling that many single men operated as sexual predators. A single woman had to be on the defensive in this area much of the time. This was deeply resented by those present. Across the country, many women have told me that this fear causes them to refrain from any dating relationship. They don't want to be forced into a combat zone.

Financial security came up on the agenda. Some present felt that many men in their age group were looking for a woman who had a career going and was secure financially. Even though this appeared to be a threat to some men, it also was high on their priority list for some reason.

Most of those present felt they had cycled through the dating world and were no longer interested in terminal relationships of one-evening duration. It took too much emotional energy and bordered on playing a game. A few felt that too many men in this instance just spent the evening talking about their ex-wife or other women they had dated. It was history-giving rather than history-making!

All the women seemed to feel they would be happy to remarry if the right person were to appear in their life. One person stated that she was now looking for *qualities* in a man rather than *qualifications*. Companionship and respect were high on the list of desired male qualities. All felt that they could not remarry a man who was still living through his divorce and had not had the years alone to grow and travel the road of self-discovery. All stated with firm conviction that their happiness was not tied to remarriage and that they were living and enjoying life in the present.

Family

Families continue to happen in the postdivorce years. We said earlier that you don't divorce your family, although a family does take on a different caste in the after-divorce years. All the women present talked freely about their children and the importance they played in their lives. Some talked about the long struggle of the years they spent alone in child-raising. No one was willing to give up any rights to their children now that they had endured the years. This was very evident when nearly all agreed that they would not marry anyone that their children did not approve of. And many of their children were married and had their own families. Children's approval of a potential marriage partner was as important as their own approval.

One woman who had lost her mate by death stated that she would like to remarry so that her grandchildren would have a grandfather. I wondered later if a sign saying "Wanted: Loving Grandfather for Exciting Grandchildren" would attract anyone. Again, the message is "I want someone to share in my life, not rule and dominate it."

Some of those present expressed the recurrence of loneliness when the last child moved out. In effect it was like another divorce, except that this time it was more haunting. I think I know why many people over the years have told me they were thankful they had children when they got divorced: They can be a weight sometimes, but at other times they can be a much-needed comfort zone. An empty nest to a married couple can be a blessing because it gives them more time for each other. To an already-single parent, it can be a yawning chasm echoing an empty life. Those responding to this agreed that the answer was to refill their lives with meaningful things and continue the journey.

Career

Recently a single woman told me that single women find careers after a divorce while men simply find other women. I'm sure that is true for some men and women, but not all. Many women are forced to economically support a family after a divorce. They often go back to school for further education, enter the job market, find out they can make a living, and gain new feelings of independence. Many who were told they "couldn't" discovered they "could."

All in our group had developed careers, but some were at a terminal point in them and were ready for new changes. The fear of change was evident, yet the challenge of new growth was stronger. No one seemed ready to become a settler. The pioneer spirit was still strong after many years of being single again. No one considered how her career or career change would affect potential male relationships. Each had developed a freedom to be her own person, and that was now an accepted part of her life. Most did admit that their careers had saved them from the need to be rescued by a man.

Ruts

Someone wisely said that a rut is a grave with the ends kicked out. A few in our group confessed to being in a rut. All seemed to agree that changes of significance can eliminate ruts in your life. A rut is doing what is easiest and what causes less fear in your life. A risk is moving out of your rut and getting sweaty palms again. A word of caution in getting out of your rut: Don't simply exchange your rut for somebody else's. As we mentioned elsewhere, watch out for the messiahs of rut removal.

Singles' Groups

I spend a great deal of my time traveling around the country telling leaders how to start and implement singles' groups. I believe in such groups deeply. All the women in our group had been a vital part of a singles' group for a number of their postdivorce years. Most had been in significant leadership roles. All talked about how the groups had helped them grow and where they were now in relationship to those groups. Several things came out.

The first was that singles' groups are largely emergency rooms for newly separated, divorced, and widowed people. They provide the care needed to heal hurts and provide a reentry to the world of singleness. All the women said they did not know where they would be today without the group that was there for them in their crisis.

A second thought was that singles' groups not only provide emergency care, but they provide a point of stabilizing and reorganizing your life. They provide structure, friendships, social outlets, and leadership opportunities. In the first two or three years of single-againness, they are vital to your survival.

A third thought expressed by our group was that you can outgrow your group and need other things in your life. You get tired of hearing divorce stories and playing dating games. You yearn for some balance and a different social catalyst for your life. You want to be with the growing people more than the hurting people. You are thankful for having the group when you needed it, but now you want to move on.

There may well be an undiscovered dimension in singles' groups that ultimately can meet this need. I have heard it expressed by hundreds of people across the country who have been single again longer than five years. Perhaps the key is going from playing the game to developing a game plan. Maybe it's a natural process of growing up in singleness, much as one goes from childhood to adolescence to adulthood. Doorways are needed in our lives, not to lounge in, but to pass through.

Remarriage

Two strong words came out of our group regarding remarriage: *fear* and *selectivity*. There are probably a few more words that you could add to this list. Fear seemed to center on the risk of a second marriage ending like the first. No matter how long ago the divorce was, in some women the fear was still strong. I don't think there is any way you can eliminate all fear other than by trusting God to help you do it and building your human confidence and self-worth to the point where fear takes a backseat.

Fear can also be a positive caution signal to us that we are not ready for something, including remarriage.

Personal fear of inadequacy also loomed large in the group. It can well be that the longer a person is out of a marriage, the more inadequate he or she can feel about marriage.

Selectivity in thinking about remarriage possibilities seemed to be greater the longer one had been single again. It is easy for the list of things you would like in another person to grow the longer you have been single. Selectivity is also contingent upon your own growth and feelings of personal self-worth. As one person said to me recently, "I want someone I don't have to drag along."

Many marriages fall apart because of a lack of growth parallels. Too often I have heard someone say, "He or she just outgrew me." Growth has to be monitored in a life. Healthy people want someone to grow with, not beyond or behind. Single-again people want a person who can share their needs, not meet them. One of the women in our group summed up her feelings by saying, "I would never want to remarry a person unless I could improve the quality of his life and he could improve the quality of my life." To me that denotes a healthy and growing person who wants to be a contributor rather than a contribution in someone's life.

Dependence Versus Independence

Personalitywise, the die for most of us was cast years ago when we were born. We collected all those genes, inherited traits, foibles, etc. and started our journey through life. Most of us fell into one of two categories: dependent or independent. We learned how to work them to our best advantage. Neither is right or wrong, good or bad; they are just different. However, they do dictate how we relate to other people and to ourselves. Dependent people who go through a divorce may tend to remarry rapidly because of their inherent need to lean on someone. Independent people can easily choose to go their own way after divorce and survive with no apparent help. Dependent people who slowly become independent through their own growth may become very selective relationally in the postdivorce years.

When they make the discovery that they do not have to lean on another person to survive in life, their new individuality can make all the leaners around them very nervous.

In the past ten years I have witnessed a new breed of survivors of the divorce experience. These are the people, both men and women, who do not race into remarriage but set apart time for an analysis of their own life and what they want from the remainder of it. They don't spend their time on a relational collision course running from singles' group to singles' group. They often look inward as well as upward in their process of becoming a renewed person. They know that they hold the key, with the help of God, to their own life. And they choose to unlock that life first.

I have watched many of these people struggle through their valleys and hurting times only to emerge a strong survivor of the divorce wars. By their own admission they are not beyond moments of loneliness, fear, and doubt; they just know they will have a good and full life whether they remarry or not.

Here is part of a letter I received recently from a survivor. It graphically sums up the thoughts, feelings, and intensity of the struggle to live beyond divorce.

> It has been a motley experience through the years, so far as wanting and hunting for a partner goes. After you begin to mend a bit you go through a period of looking and feeling that you can be a wife again. But a woman my age finds out that all the guys her own age are chasing the 40-year-olds. There aren't many fellows our own age, and most of what

there are fall into the category of creeps. When you've been married to a cultured, talented man you don't want just any old clod.

So after a while you swing between your continued need for somebody to talk to—to share joys, activities, the garden, and life in general—and your growing realization that you are becoming more and more set in your ways of living alone and doing your own thing when you want to. You begin to worry if you are becoming selfish in some respects. You begin to wonder if you could handle being married again—you know, all the extra work, the responsibilities, having to bend to somebody else's likes and dislikes again, the fear of whether you could merge lifestyles with somebody whose habits have been different from yours for more than half a century. It scares you into trying to convince yourself that maybe you don't want to remarry after all. And yet the loneliness and need for sharing, for touching and being touched is still there. The struggle is intense.

Meanwhile, you aren't finding anybody anyhow, and that only adds to your desperation. You find yourself sometimes inclined to accept caresses or handholding from a fellow single whom you really don't have all that much knowledge or affection for simply because you need it. And this worries you too. You sometimes ask yourself, "What sort of a person have I become? Am I the sport of circumstances? Am I going down the drain? I have had so many disappointments, so many failed romances for one reason or another, so many flurries—could I ever settle down to one person again?" And yet you feel that you really could, if you found someone who had the qualities you needed, who was the right personality and commitment—someone with whom you actually felt comfortable emotionally and otherwise.

But as the years begin to pass, you sink into a sort of self-defensive depression about the whole thing.

Maybe you won't ever find anybody. Or if you do, it will probably have to be a much older man. That is hard, because I am not really attracted to older men. The idea of marrying one is sort of like the thought of going to bed with my father. I struggle with the problem, back and forth. Reality is stark. Probably that is my only chance. But what if I marry an older man and it is just sort of a convenience relationship and I am not really all that happy...and then someone younger who is attractive to me comes along? It is a haunting fear. I do not believe in divorce. I would be stuck. I am afraid. Alone.

Perhaps we would have come up with another 30 things if we would have had another five hours to talk. My feeling in driving away from these eight women at the end of the evening was to give them a cheer. I have been along with them on their journey for the past ten years. I have watched their anger, their relief, their sadness, their family frustrations, their hesitancy and their healing. I have watched them climb their mountains, often alone. I have celebrated their successes and promotions and even a retirement.

They are special people who have chosen life and are living it beyond divorce. They are discovering how to turn some of the question marks of their life into exclamation points!

To Think About...

1. Do you feel that single again men and women understand each other? Why or why not?

2. As a single woman, would you give up a career for marriage?

3. How do you feel about singles' groups and the role they can play in your life?

4. Concerning remarriage, which word do you most identify with and why? *Fear* or *selectivity*?

5. Does the thought of remarriage cause you fear of losing independence? Why or why not?

Chapter 11

Beyond Divorce
As a Man

After talking to numerous men and women about the concepts of these two chapters, I have a secret wish which will no longer be secret after I tell you about it. I would like to put all the individual men and women whom I have talked with in the same room for four hours and let them express to each other what they have expressed to me. I believe a whole new depth of understanding would occur in the building of relationships between members of the opposite sex.

Silence broods misunderstanding. Communication of feelings, hopes, dreams, and fears opens those same doors wide and lets the fresh air of new life inside. Men and women need to talk *with* each other more instead of talking *about* each other. We would witness the building of healthier singles' support systems if this could happen.

After talking with a group of long-term single-again women, I wondered if I would hear the same things coming from the men. Here are some of the things that came up, both in groups and in single encounters with long-term single-again men.

The Best and the Worst of Single-Againness

The strongest two positives in this area seemed to be new friendships and new experiences. Many men felt that the single friends that were made on the hurting side of divorce were the closest friends they ever had in life. Hundreds of cups of coffee and late nights in restaurants seemed like the universal catalyst for these new relationships. The new friends often opened the door to the sharing of new experiences. The fear of new things was often hidden in the excitement of doing them with a new friend.

Some also confessed to the fear of facing new things after living with the familiar and predictable for so long. As one person stated, "No one gives you a script when you become single again. You write your own!"

The two most-often-expressed bad things about being single again were the loneliness and frustration of the dating process. Empty evenings and long weekends were the battle lines of loneliness. A few men even stated that having many single events to attend during those times did not always bring relief. In some cases it only intensified the empty moments. Added to this were the long years of memories of how this time was filled during marriage. Facing the loneliness was bad; thinking about other times was often worse.

Contrary to the popular belief of many women, men are generally frustrated by the dating process. Many confessed to the fear of asking a woman out only to be told "No, thank you!" The rejection experienced caused some to avoid any attempt at individual dating and to replace it with group experiences. Some men talked about the long-term process of dating one person after another in a seemingly endless search for the right person. One referred to this as "the dating marathon" that only left him feeling exhausted.

No one that I talked with seemed to fit the stereotypical male "predator" that many women feel are roaming the singles scene. All seemed cautious and wary and wished the process once gone through in teenage years did not have to be repeated in their forties, fifties and sixties. The one word that loomed largest in the dating area was *caution*. It doesn't need any interpretation.

Expectations

Have you ever tried shopping at your local supermarket without a shopping list? Either you forget to buy what you really need or you buy everything you don't need. Sensible people make up a list before they leave home and follow it once they arrive at the store.

Shopping lists came up a few times when we talked about dating and potential remarriage. These lists did not contain items like Wheaties, butter, bread, and eggs. These columns often contained words like Talented, Good Communicator, Good Cook, Career-Oriented, Attractive, Sports-minded, Fun-Loving, etc. etc. Most men confessed to having at least a mental shopping list when they thought of the kind of person they wanted to date and perhaps ultimately marry. I was rather amused when one man told me he had a long list but he threw it away the minute he met someone he liked. Some others said they did the same thing, but after dating the person for a time they pulled the list out and added more to it.

We all have expectations, and those expectations can become people-shopping lists in our lives. My experience would say to keep a short but well-thought-through and well-defined list. The longer one remains single, the longer the list can become. You simply have more time to make comparisons, and it is easy to go in search of the perfect person. Remember one thing when you think you have found that person: He or she also has a list!

One man in speaking about expectations said, "I only know one thing. I don't want what I've already had." The danger of this attitude is that sometimes one finds himself (or herself) comparison-shopping. I'm not sure there is a way to win in using that system.

Why Haven't You Remarried By Now?

There are two kinds of questions—those you ask yourself and those you ask other people. Perhaps a third kind is the questions that other people ask you. In dealing with thoughts on remarriage, the first kind of question was the toughest to answer. Those who responded to why they hadn't remarried listed three basic things: 1) The fear of failure of another marriage; 2) I can't seem to find the right person; and 3) I'm not ready yet.

From my experience, all three are very valid reasons. Fear of failure and the ability to take risks has to be confronted before a person can think about remarriage. A person's future cannot be viewed in the rearview mirror of the past. The past contains lessons for learning. The present and the future are a place to practice those lessons. Fear is justifiable if it is used as a teaching experience. If it is a block to growth, it has to be removed.

Finding the right person is vital to a happy relationship. It takes time, personal growth in yourself, an adventuresome spirit, and the belief that God can give you the right directions. It also means that you are to keep your eyes open.

I admire single-again people who can honestly admit that they are not ready for remarriage. In divorce recovery we teach people that it takes a minimum of two years before you are ready to even date someone and feel good about it. It takes more like three or four years before you are ready for remarriage. Many people want to take exception to this time frame, and I realize that some have done it successfully. It is not so much the days and hours as it is the maturity and settling that needs to take place in a person.

Some men (and women too) feel that they are not ready for remarriage even after seven or eight years of singleness. They have set growth objectives that they have not fulfilled, and they don't want to compromise that growth. That upsets many people who live on a contingency basis and have disposable goals. It takes a great deal of inner strength to admit that you are ready or not ready for remarriage. If you question this, go back and reread Chapter 8, "Learning to Wait."

The Older Man / Younger Women Syndrome

I could hardly wait to ask the question, "Why do older men want to date and often marry younger women?" I am asked the question everywhere I speak to groups of singles. I developed my own ideas but I wanted to hear the reasons from the men themselves.

Three things came up in response to this. The first was that dating a younger woman made a man feel more macho, self-assured and still able to be the conqueror.

The second response involved a return to youth through the company and life of another person. It is easy to feel like you want a second trip through youth when you approach your fortieth or fiftieth birthday and your friends all make jokes about your being over the hill or even under it. To a certain degree, many people live snatches of their life through other people. It can mean an instant new identity. A midlife crisis can leave a person grasping for a new identity that will relieve the crisis. Too easily it comes in the form of a younger person. It is a wise man (and woman) who can say, "I don't want to go backward. I've already been there!"

The third thing involved the ego of a man saying, "Look what I caught! I'll bet you can't catch one." Some men seemed to feel that a younger woman on the arm of an older man should have a sign attached to her with the word **COLLECTIBLE** in easily readable form.

Some years ago I remember asking a friend of mine why he always dated women his own age rather than younger women. He was about 40 at the time. His response was, "I've already raised my children." He eventually married someone his own age and has lived happily ever after.

I'm sure there are another 50 reasons yet to be shared in this strange dating and mating pattern. In all ages, many men will drop down ten to fifteen years under their age in dating and often in remarriage. And many of these marriages are happy and successful. It is simply a hard reality to face when you are a 50-year-old woman and you are being asked out by a 70-year-old man. I don't expect the trend to change in the immediate future.

Singles Groups: Why Men Don't Come

In the average singles' group, where the ages run from 35 to 55, women outnumber men from three to one to ten to one. I have asked a number of single men why this happens. Several things were expressed.

First, there were few men in leadership capacities. Men do not frequent groups where women are in charge.

Second, the program was more designed with women-type things than things that interest men.

Third, expectancies were placed upon men that they could not fulfill. An example of this was expressed by one man who said he felt he could not express his hurts and wounds and emotions to the women in his group because "big boys were not supposed to cry and express feelings." He felt a roadblock in expressing his humanity and was forced to cap his emotions.

A fourth reason that was shared can be summed up in the statement that women by nature are more relational than men. Men by nature are more vocational than women. I believe this is changing dramatically in our society as more women take on vocations and more men learn that sharing in supportive structures and close relationships is not a sign of weakness but a sign of strength. Many of the roles that we live out in society were forced upon us by other people. Roles change when we learn to carve out our own.

Many men were affirming of the role that singles' groups had played in their new lives. They felt it provided a forum for building a new network of friends and a place to share their questions, struggles, and joys. One person expressed the thought that a good singles' group was very similar to an Alcoholics Anonymous group because the people were there for themselves and for others.

I Wish Women Would...

I asked numerous single-again men to fill in the above statement from their own experiences. There were three primary responses that kept coming back.

First, many men wished that women would not have unrealistic expectations of them. To some, this meant that they did not want to be thought of as the white knight, the problem-solver, the local bank, or the answer man. First and foremost they wanted to be accepted as they were, with no precast roles or expectations.

Second, they wanted women to be patient with them and allow them to stretch, struggle, and grow. Some felt that women expected them to have it all together all the time. They also stated that they did not want to be pushed into marriage and in fact were very fearful of it.

A third feeling, closely akin to the second, was that they be allowed a spirit of vulnerability. Few felt that they were of the fortress variety. They had weaknesses and strengths and wanted to express both.

Some men felt that women took off in the opposite direction when they expressed fears and frustrations. As one so pointedly stated, "Let me out from behind my wall!"

A final concern was that women would quit viewing single-again men as prospects and look at them as persons. The feeling of forever being on display as a candidate for remarriage caused many men to run for cover, bury themselves in their career, or pursue an endless list of hobbies.

Passing Through the Doorways

Being single again for six to ten years allows a person to pass through many doorways. In listening to many people express their journey, I came up with my basic seven doorways that were most frequently expressed by the men I talked with.

The first was simply labeled Frustrations. The challenge was admitting that they existed in the single-again experience and then setting out to solve them. The list of basic frustrations varied from person to person.

The second doorway was acknowledging the need for a cooling-down or cooling-off period in those first years beyond divorce. Some admitted that they just charged ahead and found that the cooling-down time came after a number of years. It was time to rethink, retool, reevaluate, renew starting from the inside of a life to the outside. Some mentioned that they did no dating during this time because they did not want their emotional structure clouded with feelings they were not ready to resolve.

The third doorway dealt with loneliness. It is probably the most universal feeling to all people, not just single-again people. The secret in dealing with it lies in a person's ability to turn loneliness into aloneness and use it constructively to grow. Loneliness, if unchallenged in your life, will lead to self-pity and self-pity leads to depression, and you know where depression leads to. Loneliness can also be erased by building human relationships that add meaning and substance to your life.

The fourth doorway that many experienced was dealing with ineptness. Being by yourself can quickly tell you what you don't know and cause you to feel inept at what you thought you knew. It is the admission of a weakness followed by the challenge to conquer it. Single parenting and dating followed by household chores were singled out as basic areas of ineptness.

The fifth doorway involved a confrontation with bitterness. As a friend once said, "You can spend your life staying bitter or working on getting better." Bitterness is usually directed to a person and doesn't go away quickly. It often demands the process of inner healing and forgiveness. If a person is not the center of bitterness, a situation can be. We have all expressed, at least once, that feeble cry, "Why me?" The threads of bitterness, if unresolved over the years, will eventually strangle a person and render him lifeless.

Guilt filled the sixth doorway. Guilt is a boomerang of what we *did* do versus what we *did not* do. No matter how you deal with it, it keeps coming back at you. Again, the key to resolving guilt is found in forgiveness and receiving love from God and those around you. It can sometimes take a number of years to process it and resolve it.

Fear of rejection was the last doorway, and many men admitted to the fact that they were still standing in it. Rejections have a way of sticking to you. No matter how hard you try to brush them away, they are still there. As one person said, "The more acceptance you receive, the less rejection you feel."

Acceptance starts with knowing that God accepts you and loves you just as you are. You can accept yourself because God has accepted you. You can accept other people because your own base of acceptance is secure.

If you are on the "I'll do whatever I can to get acceptance" trip, you will never be accepted for what you *are*; you will be accepted for what you *do*. That's scary because when you stop doing, your acceptance level falls.

We all experience rejection from time to time. The key is in handling it, accepting it, and growing from it.

A strong desire expressed by all the single-again men that I talked with centered in the very real need for men to have women in their lives simply as good friends with no romantic strings attached. Some expressed it as a brother-sister relationship. Both the familial and Christian concept of that portrays a warm, caring, loving friendship. I have heard the same comment from single-again women whom we spoke with. Somehow that concept has to be put on the front burner in lives if people are to grow with one another. There is nothing wrong with a romantic relationship, but for many single-again men and women, their journey isn't ready to include that at the moment.

Single-again men and women have many similar feelings and needs. They need to be set free to tell each other what they are!

To Think About...

1. Share one thing you learned from the feelings that single men expressed in this chapter.

2. Share the top five items of expectations on your "shoping list."

3. Do you throw your list away when you become involved with someone? Why?

4. When someone asks you why you haven't remarried, what do you normally say?

5. How do you feel about the older man/younger woman syndrome?

Chapter 12

The Good Things in Living Alone

Earlier in this book I talked about the stages that single-again people go through in their personal growth in the land beyond divorce. The stages and transitions are natural ones. Some people go through all of them and a few more, while others hit only a scattered few of them. Unless a person remarries soon after a divorce, he or she will have to contend with a thing called single living.

Over the years of working with formerly married people, I have listened to the good and bad about single living. Often the bad seems to heavily outweigh the good, and people find themselves in an endless pursuit of escaping singleness through remarriage.

I recently spent an evening with a group of long divorced single friends in Southern California. I had one question that I wanted them to wrestle with: "What are the good things about living alone beyond divorce?" When I started the discussion, I expected a lot of joking and typical responses like "There are none. Next question!" I was pleasantly surprised when everyone tried to respond almost at once with constructive and good things about living single. The following 14 things came out of our time together. They make a good checklist for you to compare with your own feelings and thoughts.

1. *I'm free to please myself.* We all struggle with being people-pleasers and pleasers of self. To some people the thought of pleasing oneself sounds unbiblical, and, if carried to the extreme, it could be. What I heard being said in this group was that many people in their marriages had spent all their time trying to please their former spouse, and often to no avail. In the process they sacrificed themselves, and their own self-image, self-love, and ego were vastly diminished. It is true that when you have spent all your time pleasing another person, it is easy to reverse your field postdivorce and become a self-consuming person. I have met a few of those in my travels. I believe there is a fine line in the growth process where a person has to do a few self-pleasing things each day in order to experience growth.

Marriage is always a sharing of the choices and options available. It is not owning them and commanding them and making another person subservient to them. I believe that many single-again people learn the balance of pleasing themselves and others during their single-againness time to the point that when they remarry, the new relationship is far more a shared experience than the first marriage. Dare I say that one can be better prepared for a second marriage than a first?

2. *I'm free to make my own decisions.* Have you ever been shopping with a person when he or she picked up an article of clothing, examined it, tried it on, and asked you what you thought about it? Do you ever wonder if your

opinion will influence his or her choice of whether to purchase it? Many of us need another opinion or two before we feel free to make a decision on our own.

In becoming single again, one of the first realities that hits you is that you have to make decisions, and that there is usually no one present to talk them over with. For a while the fear of making the wrong decision heavily outweighs the fear of making the right decision. Then, slowly, almost like a child, one learns again the joy and risk of making a decision without consultation. What was once threatening becomes exciting. Sometimes the major discovery is in finding out that you still have the capability of making decisions. In too many marriages, decision-making is a one-sided affair. I have spoken with too many people who were told in marriage that they did not know anything and could not do anything. Later, on their own, they slowly found out that neither was true.

We all need good friends to talk things over with. We need outside opinions and shared wisdom. We all need to be able to make some decisions for ourselves. We can only learn and grow from the choices we make.

I loudly heard the affirmation from this group of people that making their own decisions was exciting and that they would never again want to revert to someone else's control in this area. Good decision-making always comes through the share-and-prayer process, whether in marriage or in singleness. It does not come from one person telling another person what to do and when to do it. Decision-making control chokes the life from a person and turns him or her into a robot.

3. *I don't have to ask permission.* I remember when I started school. One of the first things the teacher told our class was that when we needed to go to the washroom during class, we were to simply raise our hand and say, "May I leave the room?"

Going to the washroom was not a group experience or a participation sport. Yet the very nature of asking your question with a raised hand let everyone else in the room know what you were going to do. A private experience was turned into a public one. I believe that some of us developed very strong kidneys in first grade. If we could have just slipped out unnoticed, it wouldn't have been so bad. By the time I got to fifth grade, I realized that everyone went to the washroom a few times a day and it was no big deal. Asking permission and making a private concern a public matter was not easy in those days. Perhaps the art of asking the teacher for permission by a raised hand has followed some of us through life. When decision-making time comes around, we raise our hand and look for someone to grant us permission.

Asking permission is closely aligned to making decisions and pleasing oneself. Any married person knows that he has asked his spouse many times if he could do something, buy something, or go somewhere. In a healthy marriage there is a naturalness to this. In an unhealthy marriage it can spell restrictiveness. Many single-again persons who have lived in restrictive marriages cannot believe the new freedom they have discovered in not having to ask permission in some area of their life. Some have shared with me that they inadvertently look around to get permission from "anyone" to do something they want to do.

Permission is often centered in control. I now realize that this is why my early teacher would not let everyone leave the room at the same time. We would have been out of her control as a group. Permission to do or not to do in a marriage can mean that one person is controlling another person. Years of control can only build resentment and basic distrust in one's human capabilities.

As I listened to our group express themselves in this area, I heard some say:

> I can discipline my children without asking permission.

I can go out when I like and come home when I like.

I can decorate my home any way I desire.

I can find a job I like.

I can start a career or change a career.

I can choose my friends instead of inheriting them.

The list would have gone on if we had had time.

The flip side of not having to ask someone permission is learning to give yourself permission. It is owning the decision-making process. It is changing the "I must or you should" to the "I can if I choose." It is assuming responsibility for myself and enjoying it.

4. *There's a growing competence in my decision-making.* Everyone in our group expressed the feeling that the more they were forced to make their own decisions, the better they became at the process. Some even expressed the fear that if they remarried, they would lose the option of making decisions. All expressed the fact that they would marry no one who wanted to be in control over them.

We talked about making decisions that ended up being wrong but learning to let that be a building block rather than a termination of decision-risking. Many people seemed to feel that they made piles of wrong decisions in the early years of their divorce. It was only as they became more confident that this process was reversed. Sometimes the early days of a divorce are known as "crazymaking days," It can be hard to make wise decisions when your heart and head are scrambled. This changes through the process of personal growth.

5. *It feels good not to hurt and distrust anymore.* "One of the good things about my single life is that the pain my marriage caused me is gone. I don't hurt anymore and I am learning to trust people again." One person said it, and many more agreed with the feeling. Growing in singleness is getting rid of the pain of the past many times.

The hurts from a broken relationship can be carried for years after a divorce unless healing is effected. When the healing takes place, pain and hurt that may have been present for years is suddenly gone. There is a feeling of release, relief, and exhilaration that is hard to put in words. When the hurting stops, new life begins.

Hurt is often centered in a person. When that person is removed as a primary focus of life, the hurt can be healed. The entire divorce-recovery process is designed to turn the pain of divorce into gain in personal growth. We all know that there are easier ways to grow than through divorce, but if you have to *go* through it, you can choose to *grow* through it.

The question looms on the horizon, "Can I be hurt again?" The answer is definitely *yes*. There are no guarantees against hurt in life. But we can learn from what we have experienced and handle the process better in our present and future.

6. *I have a growing sense of individualism.* The expression of personhood is vital to human survival. The containment of personhood causes death to the soul and spirit. Personhood is expressed in a growing sense of individualism. It is saying, "I am a person! Do not fold, bend, staple, stamp, or mutiliate me." In the words of another participant that evening, "I am not married, I am not single, *I am a person.*" As a person, I can express my personhood through being an individual.

Being an individual is:

> Not letting others put me in a box
> Not always being predictable
> Letting the inside of me come outside
> Expressing my talents and giftedness
> Stretching beyond my capacity
> Letting others be individuals
> Thanking God for the gift of being me!

7. *My identity is not hinged to or absorbed by another person.* Identity is knowing who you are, not letting others tell you who you are. A healthy identity is not being hinged to another person who infuses his identity into you. A healthy identity is not being so absorbed by another person that you never can clearly define who you are.

Marriage is the building of two identities in a side-by-side relationship. It is not the elevation of one and the sublimation of the other. Many people in our group spoke of the loss of their identity in the years they were married and a further loss of it after divorce. Some admitted that it took them years to find out who they really were and then to feel comfortable with that person. Many people get married hoping they will discover, through marriage, who they really are. And I could not deny that a healthy marriage relationship can help in that discovery and development. When two people are open, honest, and vulnerable to each other in their growth, both will gain. The tragedy is that many marriages are one-dimensional or fall victim to the societal identities placed upon them. A good example of this is the feeling that "husbands do that" and "wives do this."

Few marriages of the eighties will survive with that kind of typecasting. Shared responsibilities work better than the role-casting ones from yesterday's world. (Yes, I do believe that the Bible sets down the job description for the roles of husbands and wives.) The key is taking it from the Bible pages and putting it into reality.

One of the strongest statements I have heard from many of my friends living beyond divorce is, "I finally found out who I am, and I like myself." That's a growth affirmation.

8. *I'm free to know my family.* Single parents are often caught between two worlds in relating to their children. Either they are not there enough for them or they are there too much for them. The secret in single parenting is to find a balance, not so much in the quantity of time given

to children but in the quality of time. When you are a single parent, you can find that the intensity of parenting is a lot higher than in a two-parent household. This can pay great dividends in the area of getting closer to your children.

Two-parent households can have a tendency to pass the children and their problems back and forth with little resolution of their needs or problems. In a one-parent household there is no one to pass the problems to, so you deal directly with the day-to-day realities. When you struggle up close to a child, you know the child a lot better. I know that the burden also intensifies, and that single parenting can become one long, tiring process. But the rewards of deeper intimacy with one's children are worth the tiredness.

9. *There's no reflection for me to mirror myself in.* We are taught quite early in life to play make-believe games. We dressed up in our parent's old clothes and pretended we were them. We went to movies and came out playing the part of the screen hero. We grew up thinking that we were the Lone Ranger part of the time and Cinderella the remainder. We tried to become the reflected image of our heroes, whether from the movie screen, the sports pages, down the street, or in our own home.

There is nothing basically wrong with trying to find a role model for your life. Most of us are the composite of many such models in our lifetimes. A problem does appear, though, when we try to be something we are not. Many single-again women shared that they felt they were mirror reflections of "the perfect housewife and mother" or their partner. When the mirror was removed, the reflection vanished and they found themselves on the self discovery-voyage without the mirror. In other words, you cannot get a healthy identity by stealing it from your mirror. As one person said, "Being single is looking in that mirror and seeing *you*."

10. *The key to happiness in progressive singleness is in my*

own growth. All the people in our group of 12 had an assortment of positive things to say about their own growth since their divorce. Some even dared to say that they would not have grown as much if they not gone through the divorce experience. You might add your "me too's" to that!

Healthy growing singles tend to agree that real happiness always comes from within, and that the key to it is in getting yourself on the road to personal growth.

The journey into growth is a long one and sometimes a slow one. It reminds me of traveling the turnpikes in the East and Midwest. When you start from New York City, there is a little sign that says Mile 1. You look on the map and see that there are 400 more of those ahead of you before you get to Buffalo! Counting them one by one as they go by makes for a long, boring journey. Looking up every hundred miles seems to make the journey go a lot faster. Growth is like reading the mileposts: They go by ever so slowly, but you know you are getting somewhere. And when you get there, you never forget where you have come from!

It is easy to be single, living beyond divorce, but not growing. It is easier to stay where you are than to start out on a new journey. A few people even start the new journey but eventually abandon it after a few mileposts. I always get excited when I see someone celebrating where they are in their single journey rather than mourning their experience. The celebrators make the journey easier for the more fearful!

11. *My security does not come in finding another person.* We live in a security-oriented society. We now have the option to live out our lives behind security-guarded communities that admit outsiders only by invitation of insiders. Jobs are designed to make people so secure that they will never leave. We all need security in different forms and doses. It is a staple in life for all of us.

The big trouble for many single-again people comes

when they want to give the job for their personal security to another person. Sometimes it comes in the form of "If I could only find someone to take care of me." It can come in the form of a release from loneliness in another person. It can take on a financial dimension. The agenda for security is a long one.

The struggle in singleness is to find security within yourself. This doesn't mean that you will never need other people, but it does mean that you start with yourself and become resourceful in learning to feel and be secure. It is tapping the well within you and reaching down deep for your own resources. It is not looking over your shoulder for the person who can do it for you. Doing it yourself can bring a refreshing shower of pride and self-worth back into a dry life.

Security is putting your trust in God for direction and decision in your life. It is allowing Him to bring forth what is often buried deep within you.

12. *I'm learning self-control.* Self-control is the toughest control room in the world to operate. At times it's overwhelming. You wish you could put the switches and buttons of your life into someone else's hands and let him take control. A few people even try this, only to realize that a person is responsible for himself.

Some areas of the battles of self-control in singleness are attitudes, anger, sexuality, physical considerations (appearance, looks, weight), relationships, children, and family. You can add your own areas to this list. Hopefully you will have won some of the battles. Like some of the already-mentioned things, self-control comes from within. It never comes by letting someone tell you what to do or doing it for you.

Self-control finds its best center in God's control. Sometimes it is simply telling God that things are out of or beyond your control and that you need His help in regaining control of the situation. He gives insight, direction, and wisdom. As you allow God to control you, I believe that your self-control will increase dramatically.

13. *Being wanted is more important than being needed.* We have all had someone express to us that we were needed. That's a good feeling because everyone needs to be needed. The problem comes when we go shopping with our "needs list" trying to find someone who will fulfill all of them. Some singles in our group felt that they had gone through stages where *their* needs were foremost in their lives. A confessed need was finding someone to fill the gap in their life. Growth in this area for many seemed to come when they knew they were simply wanted more than needed by another person. Need seems to place demands on both parties, while want is an open acceptance without the shopping list.

I am not sure that I know how to interpret this statement further. Perhaps it is one of those rare comments that needs no interpretation because everyone knows what it means. Everyone in our group nodded agreement when it was spoken.

14. *I don't see many marriages around me that I would give up my singleness to experience.* I came away from our evening group with this comment ringing in my ears. I also came away hoping that no single person would ever say that about my marriage. It was both a challenge to me and a perplexity. I wondered about the marriages that single-again people were witness to. I wondered if they were not too harsh in their judgment, or if they were simply saying, "Hey, give me a model to shoot for!" Or were they saying that they simply would not settle for second-best if they chose remarriage?

I don't think this statement is a put-down of marriage; I think it is a challenge to improve the visible models that exist. It can also say to many single-again people, "I want something a lot better than what I had the first time."

In sharing these 14 things that we talked about, I have no desire to convince anyone that singleness is golden and that those who have not remarried after a number of years beyond divorce have found a secret Utopia. It was their desire to share how they had grown, what they have felt and experienced, and to maybe say along with the apostle Paul, "I have learned in whatever state I am, to be content" (Philippians 4:11).

There are some good things that happen in the land beyond divorce!

To Think About...

1. What do you enjoy most about living as a single person?

2. What do you dislike most about living as a single person?

3. What major changes have you made in your life living as a single person?

4. How do you handle the "I need someone" versus the "I don't need anyone" feeling?

5. How have you grown in accepting some of the good
   things listed in this chapter.

Chapter 13

Am I Ready
for Remarriage?

Are you ready for remarriage if the opportunity comes your way? There are probably three answers to that question: Yes! No! Later! The first question is usually followed by a second: "How do you know when you are really ready for remarriage?" The answer is really individual and highly contingent upon where a person is in his or her own life.

I have put together 46 questions that may help you get a little edge on knowing where you are. This test is far from an authoritative final word; it is a simple guideline based on talking with thousands of formerly married people as they have trekked through the land beyond divorce.

The "Am I Ready for Remarriage" Test

1. Have I dealt with forgiveness in the area of my former spouse?

2. Have I really experienced a healing in the area of hurts caused by my divorce?

3. Am I still playing "get even" games with my former spouse?

4. When someone asks me about my divorce, do I have a hard time recalling the events and situations?

5. Do I think of myself as a divorced person?

6. Has my self-esteem grown measurably over the past three years?

7. Do I enjoy my work, vocation, career?

8. Do people tell me that they can't believe how well I'm doing?

9. Am I always looking for a potential mate everywhere I go?

10. Would I rather go out with girls (or guys) than on a single date?

11. Am I haunted by loneliness in my life?

12. Do I enjoy making decisions for myself?

13. Am I glad there is no one there when I come home at the end of the day?

14. Do I enjoy going to singles' groups?

15. Do I resent the word "single?"

16. Am I envious when I see other happily married people?

17. Can I measure my growth in the years since I became single again?

18. Am I looking for someone to take care of me?

19. Am I looking for someone to take care of?

20. Do I feel that the person I might remarry has to be accepted and liked by my children and family?

21. Do I enjoy hearing other people's divorce war stories?

22. Do I believe I will make a good wife or husband for someone?

23. Do I still largely fear remarriage?

24. Do I feel comfortable with my singleness?

25. Am I excited about possible career advancements or changes?

26. Do I usually wait for someone to tell me what to do?

27. Am I angry that I am single at this point in my journey through life?

28. Am I still bitter about my divorce?

29. Do I feel good about my personal growth and accomplishments?

30. Do I make plans and work toward goals in my life?

31. Do I think that all men (women) have a hidden agenda in remarriage?

32. Do I believe I am lovable?

33. Do I believe I can be a contributor to the happiness of someone else?

34. Am I a happy person?

35. Do I believe that God really loves me and has forgiven me for my divorce regardless of what other people might think?

36. Is my lifestyle mergeable?

37. Do I have a "who-needs-you" feeling toward the opposite sex?

38. Is the thought of remarriage an exciting challenge or a calculated risk?

39. Am I willing to invest a year or two in building a relationship that could lead to marriage?

40. Would I feel safe with a prenuptial agreement?

41. Have I worked through my biblical concerns with the issue of remarriage?

42. Can I live happily ever after if I do not choose remarriage?

43. Do I believe there is only one person out there for me, and if I miss him or her, that's it?

44. Do I believe I am a loser if a long-term relationship does not end in marriage?

45. Have I traded in my "Happiness Is Being Single" shirt for one that says, "Happiness Is Being Human!"?

46. Have I grown in my relationship with God? Is He real and vital in my life?

Every test demands some sort of grade. We are always eager to know if we passed or failed. If you answered the following questions according to what I have observed, you are well on the way to growing and being prepared for remarriage.

YES on 1,2,4,6,7,8,12,14,17,20,22,24,25,29,30,32,33,34, 35,36,39,40,41,42,45,46.
NO on 3,5,9,10,11,13,15,16,18,19,21,23,26,27,28,31,37, 43,44.

A word of caution: Please don't take your test results to the next singles' meeting you attend and set your table by the door under a sign, "All offers gratefully considered!" If your score was good, just smile a lot and know you have *grown!*

POSTSCRIPTS

No book contains everything a person hopes will lie within its pages. There are many areas in living beyond divorce that we have touched upon lightly or not even at all. To cover everything would mean talking to everyone and producing a 20-volume set of books. I have tried to be practical, inspirational, motivational, and biblical—a tall order to fill for someone who is still learning!

Several affirmations have emerged in this writing that I want to reemphasize.

1. You are God's unique, unrepeatable miracle. You are loved by God. You are special!

2. It is more important to know that you are a person than to carry the brand of single and divorced.

3. If you allow God to be at the center of your life, living beyond divorce will be a lot easier.

4. There is nothing wrong with wanting to remarry and praying that you will. There is nothing wrong with wanting to remain single and praying that you can.

5. God is not on your timetable. You are on His!

RECOMMENDED READING

Hocking, David. *Good Marriages Take Time.* Eugene, OR: Harvest House Publishers, 1984.

Hocking, David. *Marrying Again.* Old Tappan, NJ: Fleming H. Revell, 1983.

Juroe and Juroe. *Successful Stepparenting.* Old Tappan, NJ: Fleming H. Revell, 1983.

Krantzler, Mel. *Learning to Love Again.* New York: Crowell Co., 1977.

Richards, Larry. *Remarriage: A Healing Gift from God.* Waco: Word Books, 1981.

Small, Dwight Hervey. *The Right to Remarry.* Old Tappan, NJ: Fleming H. Revell, 1975.

Smoke, Jim. *Every Single Day.* Old Tappan, NJ: Fleming H. Revell, 1982.

Smoke, Jim. *Growing Through Divorce.* Irvine, CA: Harvest House, 1976.

Smoke, Jim. *Suddenly Single.* Old Tappan, NJ: Fleming H. Revell, 1982.

Visher and Visher. *Stepfamilies: A Guide to Working with Stepparents and Stepchildren.* New York: Brunner-Mazel, 1979.